Spoor
of an
Indian Horse

Soman Gouda is a writer, filmmaker and poet from India. His enduring fascination with the films and spirituality inspired his first non-fiction work, a philosophical essay, 'Yogi in Suits', which came into limelight in a very short span of time and garnered international acclaim.

Soman admires Gibran, Ruıni and Tagore's poetry, 'Seedlings of Light' is his first haiku collection. His feature-length film 'Mocktale' received a rave response and appreciation from the audience. He also published 'Gulabi Kode', a short story collection in kannada. All in all, Soman is an emerging creator of art from India with maverick perspectives and genuine insights.

Spoor of an Indian Horse

A Novel

Soman Gouda

SomeKranthi Creations
Bengaluru, India

SomeKranthi©
India
Published by SomeKranthi Creations
16/2, 3rd Floor, Muniswamappa Road, Halasuru,
Bengaluru 560008, Karnataka, India
Mob: 9985007590
somekranthi@gmail.com

SomeKranthi Creations
Bengaluru, India

ISBN: 9788193727263

First impression 2020

Chapter 1

"Never do you attempt to lick my wounds. Your profuse commiserations mean nothing but a babble of an insane to me. Look at yourself. You are blind to the obvious, blind to your own blindness. Your life is a masticated chewing gum. You continue to spit it into your quivering cupped hands and then swallow it back blatantly as though it's a prasadam, the god's mercy — a perpetual nausea. You have no courage or the conviction to discard it and start anew. In precise, you are a milksop," she had averred, along with the hammering whistle of a hitherto conspicuous Nepali Gurkha, in the dead of that night. 'We were prepared for the tides of full moon but not for the tsunami,' whispered those meek spectators, the walls, as she strode out like an angry whirl of a cyclone, slamming the door of her heart. Her capriciousness has got all the merits to beat the erratic rains of the monsoon and the frenzy volatility of stock exchanges. The same walls, my all weather friends, uphold my opinion till the ceiling, about her vagaries. Though in looks are plane and even, they are pregnant with the truth. Those are the only beings that seem to have witnessed my naked soul and thus possess the honor to advocate on my behalf. Nonetheless, they appear to be overwhelmed and came to a private consensus — to be on a self imposed vow of silence. Thus, I am obliged to voice their emotions.

I have come to believe that my story is one of the greatest of this epoch, as significant as Anne Frank's for the last century. Lest my fellow humans choose to snub it as an embroidery, the kind history won't. I have a deep-rooted faith in humanity. I don't remember when was it that I decided to descend my half-baked fairy-tale like life through a disobedient pen on to the processed silvers of a dead tree.

Like an ethereal scent of an anonymous lady in the elevator that engulfs our perception and succeeds to befuddle the thought process, some set of words exert a profound impact, so much so that one tends to forget who uttered them and when. They are the words that echo in the deepest well of the self —

"All that you write about memories is fiction. The person, who glances at them objectively, is awfully different than the one who experienced. Can you be as pure, unsullied and innocent as the experiencer? You incline to keep enhancing and dramatizing those experiences based on your current worldview and imaginative capabilities. When you essay to be subjective or say you want to relive them, they slip through your fingers like the water flowing in stream. They call you from the other shore, your childhood memories, there's an inexorable flux runs between you and them which you can't grasp or perforate. Memories are elusive. They are the imaginations with the colors of reality. Never trust those deceptive silhouettes behind the translucent windows..."

It must be her, my 'golden-hour friend' whom I used to chance upon in the morning and evening walks. She had also added that "No autobiographies bear the unvarnished truth, for there is nothing called truth. If there is any, it's inexpressible." I had stood in stupefaction attempting to appraise her forthright attitude. She had managed to embroil me with a conundrum before leaving my room that night. My eyes were fixed at the centre of the ceiling fan and the left hand fingers fumbled on the loose knots of my thick chest-hair. Time slows down when you gaze at a ceiling fan.

"Solid blades of a fan go invisible in action. Imagine your memories," said within me, her leftover, a last piece of her soul.

Did she just dampen my spirits? Or was it a mere display of her punditry? If it's anything more, all in all, it must be her prejudice, owing to the twists and turns in her masked life. I attempted to recover my mental composure.

The focal point was all that my eyes were concerned with. Gradually, I was compelled to figure out the shape of the fan in its hereditary rotation. Those grimed blades and their sharp edges.

Earlier that day, in the subway train, a charming girl of the age of about sixteen or say seventeen, perhaps eighteen, looking into my eyes, offering her seat, had coldly uttered, "Uncle you may please get seated," I was abashed and taken aback. My face had turned red and my 'young blood' boiled. *Shades of grey in my hair and the thick horn-rimmed glasses impel me to look an uncle or am I the uncle already for real?*

"No, I am fine..." I had rebuked attempting to conceal my annoyance and private humiliation. I wiped off those beads of perspiration that glistened with agitation which were ready to take their course through the furrows of my forehead. The handkerchief, soaked with shame, found its way back to the pocket and my gaze towards the moving sky scrapers and the swaying trees through the windows. I occupied an empty seat, soon after the notorious girl and her plump friend with the elephantine thighs alighted at the next station.

There was an old man who looked like a yesteryear veteran gangster, sitting opposite to me staring sternly, as though I owed certain debts to him from past life. He carried half of his missing sleep in his heavy, swollen eye-lids. His pencil moustache, glossily plastered hair, bare chest save for the locket made with the nail of a beast resting in the sleek slope of his breast, made him look ten years younger to me.

I cradled my bag on my laps and ducked my head, to engage a glance at my palms to avoid the eye contact with any other humans in the train — like a solipsistic cat that shuts its eyes while lapping up the milk. The complex tapestry of lines in my palm and a mark of scorched pinch evoked a deep buried melancholy and a vague nostalgia. I observed the lifeline and headlines — attempted and failed to decipher my life expectancy. My eyes, driven by the impulse, turned towards the palms of a stout man sitting beside me. His left hand did not even possess any lines, and I couldn't make it to his right as it had embraced the shiny steel rod like a tight hug of a teen. I grew sentient of fleeting time. *What have I become of?* I gazed at my face in the opposite window as the train glided through underground burrows carved out by the modern man. Yes, the windows are the mirrors in darkness. Incidentally, a little girl said 'No' and agitated to take a seat next to me, though her parents urged. She threw a pale look at me with the crimsoned face and awkward eyes. As a compensatory gesture, her parents acknowledged at me with the apologetic eyes and then a scowl towards their sulky, defiant child. Those momentary mirrors must have sniggered at my misconception that 'to remain a bachelor implies-to remain young forever'.

As the train drifted further in space-time fabric, a better version of me invited a thought that *'I might get wiped off from this existence at any flash of time. I am no Sisyphus to chain up and detain the god of death. Though the events like World War III, or an attack from the aliens, or the outbreak of a terminal flu, or an asteroid collision are not imminent, I will certainly be obliterated from the face of earth. Sooner or later, I will have to get down at my station whether I want it or not. I can't remain in the train forever'*. The very next moment, in tune with the weather of Bangalore, my mind grew cloudy, and the face must have looked insipid and gloomy. There were no mirrors to check by now, all I had were the hazy windows, to see out and see far. That's when I made my mind to narrate my story.

Writing about the self after making love is even more stimulating — the process of stripping an already stripped man, the process of finding the traces of light after a grand enlightenment. I turn on my table lamp. The most meaningful device invented so far. I arbitrate with pen over the opening line, just the way I did on the other betraying night. At last I resort to the instinct, for my flunk to write the most adorable incipit.

I am not one of those who change their own names while writing their autobiographical accounts. I am Laxman. I don't have any brother with the name Rama. It's hard to ascertain why they named me after Laxman though I am their first son. My friends at work call me Lax, especially the white people. It took me many days to realize that it's a device they employ to tease me for my idling way of life — Lax. Anyways, they are proven masters in anglicizing any damn Sanskrit or Indian name into a modern sophisticated western sounding title. My old colleagues, Jagadishwara is turned to Jag and Timmareddy has become Tim. We all like this concept for the convenience it offers in business communication as it avoids many embarrassments and the comedy of errors. Well, let's keep the names and Shakespeare aside. The essence of life that I experience on weekends is poles apart with the weekdays. But if you ask me collectively, all the weekdays are the same and all the weekends are the same too. Eternal spells of run of the mill, mundanity, prosaic or whatever you name it.

Mind takes a somersault and the concentration turns into a slack bowstring which can shoot no more. I turn towards my left to find out the gap between the curtains which allows a beam of blue light from a distance to divert me, I shun it mercilessly. I don't like the bathroom door to be left ajar during the writing spells. As my left hand pulls the door handle, my shorts call me up, stained with semen, half wet, lay on sink table top. I rinse it in the sink. A weird thought flashes in my mind — this granite would get pregnant if it ever had a life.

I slump back to my writing table. All that I wrote looks pretentious, vainglorious and alien, as though written by an inferior clone of me. I endure and try to push the pen in different directions. There's no way I progress. They vanish before me without taking any concrete shapes, those silhouettes of reminiscences. As I sit helpless, gazing towards nowhere, there's something that echoes from within, a song, too faint to grasp, from an unknown past. I struggle to drift into the slumber and fail miserably. Like a grouchy dog that wriggles while being dragged into the water, I agitate. I am the dragger and the dragged. All in vain. After the groping in dark like a nocturnal parasite searching for a host, I open the curtain, a light beam hits again followed by the tempestuous wind. I must have looked blue, as blue and opaque as a sapphire on that sardonic night.

Chapter 2

'Tamarind seedling on a cow dung cake — a green phoenix.' I jotted down at an empty edge of the newspaper. Such random lines, they come when they come, like the unexpected guests on an arid afternoon. There are crude Sundays, on which the daughters go Daddies' home and the mothers to their lovers'. She had presented herself early that grey morning, precisely to make love. My shorts of the yesterday hung still damp starving for the sun and a little air.

Those blue poppies on her long milk-white tunic came to life as she got herself busy, nimbly like a meditation, serving the breakfast that she had prepared and brought for us — spicy poha, omlette and fruit salad. Her bare arms full of life glinted even in the weak light as she leaned forward to place the laden plates on teapoy. Perhaps, she was aware of my furtive glances directed at her bosom negotiating from behind the pages of *economic times*. Before long, the cutleries instigated their dialogue with those distinct clinks in a coherence and she managed to seize the moments in the gaps to explain how her mother convinced her to accept and devour off the food consignments sent with 'love and care' — rice packets, bananas, dry coconuts, pickles, Kolkata special sweets and what not.

In all of our conversations, she never looked into my eyes nor did she bother to wait for a response from me. I suppose, I did not feel subjugated for my concupiscence towards her. At times, the passion for intimacy collided with my mindfulness and steadily tapered my awareness, like a sandglass losing its space, grain by grain in time.

The bright, stark and commodious room had turned into a black-and-white interior by the mischief of sun. The pronounced streaks of sun light, through the cracks of curtain that used to fall on light-ivory tiles were on no show. She orphaned those ornate ceramic plates with leafy leftovers by forsaking them onto an already introverted wooden stool in the corner and got to her feet towards the remote of air-conditioning. I settled back to my previous composure on my unmade bed with *economic times*. Gently, as the words lost their existence, the silences lead us to the ultimate. Then, we lost and won, budded and bloomed together on the somnolent bed only to realize that its late afternoon and the sky still grey. Sun must have crawled under the balmy grey blanket like an infant's struggle to get off from the bed. A lull fell on, and the silence flooded the room again. I took a deep sigh and pretended to be falling asleep by a huddling and closing my eyes.

She departed. Like the last train of the night leaving behind the fading chugs and vibrations that lingered for long and rippled at the core of stillness.

I took my own time to get back into the conscious frame of mind. A pleasant aroma of her slender body loitered about me for a while. She was after-all a stranger few months ago. We hardly had exchanged eye contacts in our ascents and descents in the elevator and a handful of times in the park. Frankly, on a fatigue evening, I had sought a view of her cleavage secretively through the ceiling mirror in elevator.

She ran regularly in tights. My eyes felt free to overwhelm themselves with the rear end of her during the hiatus between my running spells. Her sumptuous bottoms and the venus dimples were all enough to accelerate one's horse-beat.

It was when she looked forlorn, and struggled to lift a rice packet up from the elevator landing to her flat, I was obliged to lend a hand (rather a shoulder). She accepted my offer fervently with those gladdened merry brown eyes and the bloomed cheeks. There was a touch of her finger that aroused my manliness. That spark of ignition was all that was needed for the hungry tides to kiss the moon. Then we grew organically to become the 'meaningful' neighbors, setting ourselves off into the ultimate quest of finding the meaning of life, hand in hand, and bosom on the bosom. There are two moles on her body: one on the right thigh and the other at the leftward edge of her lower lip. Both of them posed a firm challenge for me to record her body comprehensively in its entirety. Her broad and glossily voluptuous heaving bosom which could melt the mountains, and those lustrous legs as though carved out of boles of young banana trees, managed to keep the flame alive in me. 'God must have taken inspiration, rather plagiarized from the painting Crenaia, The Nymph of the Dargle while creating you' — I used to conjure up a jest conspicuously embedding my intellectual credentials into them. She responded on all of such occasions with a forceful smile and an indifferent countenance. The silence was exploited as much the words by her liaison with me.

It emerges again that I took time to escape from her hangover. I got to my feet towards the window and gazed out through the gap of curtain; the world was the same — at sixes and sevens. Stream of vehicles honked and moved in a hurry; a bunch of young fellas were absorbed in an aftereffect of a joke while they smoked and sipped juice in-front of a juice bar along the front road of my condominium; in a little distance perpendicular to the front road, a construction laborer had stretched himself on a mound of earth beside a foundation pit; a mother with a bowl in her hand was negotiating with her boy for one more morsel, chasing him about his hide and seeks through the colorful cloth-lines on a terrace.

I closed the curtain impulsively followed by a hollow sigh. It all looked like an orchestrated street mime — so theatric, so metaphoric and illusory. There are times, when the life compelled me to believe that the whole existence is a fine premeditated fiction; a fable conjured up by a reclusive artist. I tramped back towards the bed to find myself at the loose end. The consciousness evaporated for the moment and I lay down still, like a robot with the stiff neck and limbs, gazing at the bare walls, my eternal confidantes. I cut the edge off from the newspaper where I had written a line and placed the chit into the womb of my notebook. There emerges a thought on the horizon of my mind — *the life is all about picking up the pebbles from a lonely shore*. My pen grows shy and displays a strange reluctance to carve it down.

I can't establish on what seduced me for an evening stroll. Whether it was the fear of getting submerged in her thoughts or the mental chaos post the physical labor or a mere impulsive human propensity to break out from the cocoon. I hung my washed short next to the yesterday's with the remark — let it enjoy the company, and got bemused by my idiosyncrasies — the way my will works, the way my thoughts manifest, the way I react to them. Then, the pragmatism knocks the door. I rummaged through the wardrobe for my favorite shirt to step out. To wade out from the murky mood, to seek some purples in the midst of greys.

I had no shirt to school that day, hovered for a while on 'my terrace' semi-nude surveying the horizon. It had become mine by then — an old, abandoned veterinary clinic right opposite to our hut. A huge tamarind tree had canopied it partially. I remember all those scenes that my mind could capture that radiant morning: People opening their skylight windows to invite the invigorated sun into their house; smoke streams rising up from kitchen chimneys — that looked like the cigarettes of Gulliver; buffaloes and cows unclasping their limbs and joints to get ready for their graze; old and young men walking into the fields below the skyline with the scarlet and parakeet colored plastic pitchers in hand lifting their *lungies* up till their knees; few plump puppies playing cheerfully on the heap of damp sand as if they were born for jollification (I was told that if any puppy is found playing freely beside the streets, it should be female, shepherds habitually pick up the male dogs and enlist them into their herds without their consent); and then, the running bicycles that looked like miniature toys on the ring road with the backdrop of hazy blue hills.

Even, I used to pedal the cycle while my best friend Ishwar batted for a longer time. He was a 'worst batsman'. That's what everyone called him, the worst among all. He never made any runs eating up most of the overs. Nonetheless, I had attained the badge of a good fielder. They tapped my back and used to blow me up hailing me as Jonty Rhodes of the team, for I was always a fielder and never got a chance to bat or bowl. I was kind of self-contented with the fielding and enjoyed it. You never know which direction the ball springs from, one has to be eyes all the directions, like the lord Indra who had thousand eyes. Over the above, one has to run quicker than the ball to chase it in all the odd times — the glare of sun or a tiny stone in the ground could trick the fielder anytime. They subject one to ridicule if one fails to catch hold of the little sphere, and even resort to yell mercilessly if the catch of a decent batter is dropped. In the worst case, fielder would be out-casted from the group and passed over during the selection. I had witnessed it happening to couple of my peers.

That Saturday afternoon there was an important match. So important that no one seemed to display any unease or resentment for the broiling sun. The equation was such that, a boundary could change everyone's fate for that day. Akshay's team needed four runs from the last ball of the match. For my good (or bad) luck, the ball sprung towards me like an asteroid from a remote space and all the creatures present in the ground screamed my name in unison — Luckyyy. As I used to field at long-on boundary line, I didn't have a choice but to give a big dive towards my right and stop that little monster before the echo of my name faded. I did. The miracles seem to happen for those who take reasonable risks in the ripe moment. They all lifted me up for my valiant sporting spirit. A hero was born in no time. I was over the clouds. Perhaps that was my first remarkable feat in life. My name got reverberated again all through the ground, making me popular among the bristling *ashoka* trees and the crumbling walls of school. Steadily, as I brought myself back to my senses, I realized that there was a hole! Not in my heart but under the right arm. The hole that I surmised turned out to be a long rip that stretched from my armpit to the midline. The reasonable risk did not seem reasonable anymore. They all rejoiced in triumph and were thrilled as each of them won two or three bucks. I struggled hard to hide my tears and wept within for the irreparable state of my shirt, envisioning my imminent encounter with Avva and the consequent exile.

Five strokes per day if you miss the uniform. Traces of faded scars on my palms reminded me of my grumpy headmaster — the man with the grey whiskers in ears. I had tasted the fate already, at the beginning of the academic year — thirty beatings from newly carved raging cane for a week. It was not my mistake but of the tailor who delayed the delivery of my uniform. Well, it was not tailor's mistake either; it was my father who delayed paying him.

No it's not father's mistake too, mother did not sanction money to father on time. Then, is it the mistake of my mother? No... The milk consumers did not pay their bills on time, though we knocked their doors every day like vagrants. Therefore, it was the fault of our whole village and yet I was the one punished for it. All through the week, while I walked to the school, I must have empathized with myself with the thought that I must be the reincarnation of the scapegoat which was sent into the wilderness by Jewish people, laying their sins upon it.

The orange sun grew invisibly effulgent and my shirtless bulk felt the heat. Every individual cell in my body protested the unmerciful sun and my condition at the same time. There manifested a serious shadow of mine on terrace more subtle and more apprehensive. My schoolmates attired in immaculate uniform, sky blue on the top and navy blue in the bottom, marched along the road with the vigor of Indian Airforce officers without insignias. Few of them flourished their compass boxes with colorful satchels on their backs. Girls thumped their feet in the fine red clay to create the perfect and intact impressions of their shoe, to leave their footprints engraved in the backyard of my mind. I am unsure if I envied at them but my eyes combed through those blue streams in search of an odd speck, anyone at the least to stand with me, out of the line, for the cane ritual. For my despair, I found none.

My haughty seniors strode with the untucked shirts and the supercilious horns over their head and conducted themselves as though they were already passed out of school. Then emerged the girl with chicken legs — Prathibha, my sister's classmate. Everyone called her Gooseberry, as she managed to swallow them in class so surreptitiously that even her nose would have no idea of it. She had reserved an affectionate smile for me always, no matter when or where I encountered her. She ceased to visit our home since Rani left to the city. Avva, my mother offered Rani in marriage to Mantu, Avva's own younger brother. Rani's marriage was decided when she was in the womb. Marriages are made in wombs whenever the god keeps himself busy in heavens. Mantu had studied some sort of industrial training course and worked in a factory in Mumbai. They lived there happily ever after. That's what Avva assumed and tried her best to defend herself and her sovereign decision.

The very thought of Rani seemed to had done a magic for me. A window of instant revelation had unbolted in my mind to create a eureka moment. I stepped down the stairs like an Archimedes and sprung into my shack. Avva was busy preparing her lunch box — jowar roties with the topping of amber colored tamarind chutney and some green gram curry, and that's all, to light up the swarga for the day. I opened an old rather an ancient rusty trunk, the then treasure trove of our family, stealthily with utmost chariness. However, I couldn't avoid its creak reaching my Avva's already pricked ears. Mothers sense it all well, the reasons of jubilations. After fishing out two or three clothes of mother, my heart bloomed with an exclaim — there you go! Rani's shirt, the only thing that could elevate me to the seventh heaven for the moment. I held it up with its shoulders for a cursory glance. It looked neat and tidy despite its wrinkles, like an old nurse. It was evident by its resilience that there was still a lot of life left in it.

"It's Rani's," said mother from kitchen, catching a glimpse through the frame of doorway.

"I know that. You need not worry; she won't come back hoping to wear it again," I responded haughtily, ironing its collar with my hands, applying all of my triumphant strength. She was quiet as expected, since she had already had a spell of scornful reprimand towards me on the day of the match. En passant, I was not the lonely victim of her tirade but the whole cricket team and their lineages. It is mother's essential nature, she gives once but her best. She had assured me that it would be futile from my end to expect any new shirt from her at-least till the next Deepavali and that's it.

The shirt was all fine but... for my ill fortune, it had no pocket. I could escape my headmaster's cane somehow, but how about the entire class? All would ridicule me as a girlish boy. It was impossible to wear a girl's shirt — a question of sheer prestige. My brain seemed to had worked swiftly again. I stitched a new pocket to it by ripping my old torn out shirt. It's interestingly strange that one calls shirt a shirt even it's torn and shaped out. In the conclusion, I was all set to walk to school with a brand new customized shirt. The pocket looked like creative embroidery with its mosaic-like random stitches of a thick white thread. I had turned out to be an accidental artist that day. Unsure if all the art in this world is accidental. Anyways, Rani had saved me even in her absence. Perhaps that's how the world works; all the good things are done by the virtue of the gone. In the course of her departure to Mumbai, she had carried the seeds of evening jasmines *Mirabilis Jalapa* with her. We had grown and nurtured a huge bush of them around our shelter and had fenced them with countryside acacia sticks. I liked yellow and she loved pink. There were many fragrant-full evenings in our path, as we indulged ourselves in counting the blossoms of our favorite colors. Multi-hued were kept aside and we labeled them — 'for god'. I remember, Rani turning her skirt into a temporary basket to carry those flowers into the hut to prepare the garlands for the almighty.

My Avva always used to advise me not to play cricket, stating that 'it's a game of rich people' but I was the one, who failed to grasp her prophetic sense in its entirety. I never showed up to cricket again on school uniform. My shirt went on fine for some good time winding away my anguish. It had the fragrance of Mirabilis lingered all through.

Towards the sundown, I seem to grow nostalgic. I wear an imported tartan patterned flannel shirt and make my way through the crowd of Imperial Street. Like an orphan bamboo straw that floats on a wild river approaching a bend. There are perfumes of strangers — citrus and minty, fragrant and fruity those pervade my awareness. I almost forgot how it smelled, the Mirabilis. Should I walk to the flower market in search of its pepper-like seeds? Will they prosper in my apartment? Will they bloom the same way they did before years around my shack? Will they emanate the same aroma of childhood? I stand stupefied at an edge of a cross road. Before my heart vents to cross, I get drifted by the crowd towards the subway station. Sky looks orange — a concoction of yellow and pink. Somewhere down the skyline sun must have held his breath and waited. There are things left unsaid. I float and progress and eventually disappear.

"Be attentive and always have an eye on her," my mother had said before leaving to her work — weeding in the sunflower field.

Chapter 3

"One more Brain-Freezer please," she had ordered with an air of authority. To my impression, it will not be an exaggeration if I posit that we were on top of the city. Cafe Rapture, for that matter had attained all the attributes to reinforce my view. I can't establish on whose idea was it to pick out the terrace café. Though I liked open air rooftop restaurants, I favored dim lighted, poised and placid ambience where one could catch the decibels of whispers. We had opted for a corner table adjacent to the balustrade so could escape the limelight. The view of the street looked malignantly agleam with the ornate, moon-like street lamps. The flashy lights spilled out from the windows of euphoric pubs and the streaks casted by car lamps upon their faces made the strollers glisten in orange and red. Those damp cobble stones towards the end of the lane shimmered and looked like the pavement laid with the gold biscuits. To all its intents and purposes, the mysterious aura of the place had instilled a sense of lucid-dream like atmosphere to the perambulators, who generally acted on spur of the moment. On to the right, sky trains passed once in a while like the manmade comets carrying men and women between the heavens of weekends. A Honolulu creeper entwined all along the balustrade, tried to whisper something with its idiosyncratic pink intimacy. Its gentle leaves brushed my elbow recurrently provoked by the breeze. The pink of it wasn't marred by the smog created by stoners, nor did it look bleak. In the contrary, it had turned even more exuberant and scintillating. The man behind the aesthetic beauty of the ambience to his great taste for fixtures won the brownie points, irrefutably from all the visitors. As for the tables and chairs, they were timbered prudently with split logs and were painted in a combination of brilliant blue and white that complimented the vibrant nights. There were many stoned eyes piercing through the hanging wisps of smoke that hunted the oblivion. I felt dizzy at times and the cephalalgy was sowing its seeds already somewhere in the deep corner of my cranium. Many teen girls looked consummate with the hookah hoses and urbane expressions during their chatter. A sense of dejavu pulsated and disappeared as I grew outwardly conscious.

"Let's play a game," she snapped my gaze and tried her best to manufacture a sort of buoyant mood with her *nirvaanic* eyes.

"I am a sinner and you are a saint, so who am I?"

"Sinner," I threw an instant response.

"Well, so you are a sinner too."

I beheld at her eyes, sipping my mocktail — Blue Heaven. Her hookah smoke wafted towards me to nuzzle with my breath, gentler than her words.

"Calling someone a sinner is also a sin, so we both are sinners before this sinful world now, you get it?" she continued with the spirit of a college girl. Every woman seems to possess this strange quality — to traverse back and forth in the timeline of mental age. That was the first time ever I had experienced her speaking anything weightless and light hearted. It seemed out of her character and proved to be unsuitable for her demeanor. She appeared to have known it by herself, and yet she attempted. *We are all that. Some or the other time, everyone in their lives, try the unsuitable for the sake of a mere experience.* I reflected.

All those souls on that night scrambled under the open sky, wriggled to blow their melancholies and moral emotions out in the form of smoke — a gaseous catharsis. They craved to unshackle the guilt out from their rattled bosoms in the hope to become lighter, to become one with the clouds, to float around the moon like diaphanous celestial bodies. They hankered to grope with the light sitting in the darkness accumulating the marsh green mucus in their chests. I couldn't dare do it myself.

All that I had done was the surveillance from a dark corner, like a spy camera. I had travelled my gaze across all the hazy apparitions on the terrace and had strolled with the strollers in my own way, but not into her. She appeared more opaque than ever before, and I had my head in the clouds most of the time. From out of the blue, a long-lasting inquiry propped up in me like a psychedelic fountain.

'Do I mix up with all these people? My external appearance might contend for it, however, deep inside, at the core, do I really? Am I the only black sheep up here? Am I the only hat that fell on the perimeter of the ring? Part in, part out?' Before could I fathom the source of such notion, my heart vented to answer: 'I never felt one with them, I never could play it their way — the craft to forget the time and space unconsciously and get immersed in the party. I never did. I pretended whenever it turned out to be inevitable and resisted if braced by time. *One might escape the war but not the fear of it.*

Little muddled and unfulfilled, I had withdrawn from the show. Yet the question 'Did the soul of that creeper ruminate through me? Or did it try to whisper in my ears by brushing my elbow that 'dear pal we both don't belong here, but it's okay, life is all about that — to learn to belong into where you always think you don't'.

Crowned with the confusion and with a sense of emptiness, I climbed down the stairs after her, to walk on the footpath that led to MG Road subway station. It was our mutual consensus to carry ourselves separate from each other while in public, like the remote planets that revolve around a centre called emptiness. As I wended my way further, I was encountered by a disheveled lady in a torn out *saree*, with a bamboo basket over her head. She appeared to be a hawker, who sold roasted chickpeas, salted peanuts and the memories as well…

My Avva never seemed to care what I did, as long as I was compliant with two plies — looking after Kaali and my attendance at school. Though the former had more weightage in the balance scale of preferences, I had to maintain the equilibrium of both, like as they say in modern terms: work and life balance (So work is not life?). I always used to assume that my school was built only for my advantage, for it was a situated outskirt of the village, surrounded by fairly fragmented plots of contrasting barren lands and green farms. Also, there was adequate buffer space with the patches of green and brown grass behind the school, and beyond that were corn and sugarcane fields. Kaali used to be in good terms once in a while — she grazed by the barriers, hedges, embankments and boundary-dykes. There was a petite bronze made bell dangled under her neck. My subconscious could keenly trace her presence by the distinct tinkles of it. I kept an eye on her during the interludes, and my vigils went on from the class room window as well.

I suppose it was the last class of that sweltering day. We were all soaked in the perspiration of boredom and waited for a little air and freedom. Kaali had begun her second spell after a brief nap. I watched on her furtively, looking over my shoulder through the window. Carrying her huge bovid bulk, she had already made halfway along the hedge and was stood by a small entry way into to the farm. Her eyes were indubitably allured by the sea of lush green beyond the border as she loitered there curiously with the wiggling ears. My instinct said, she is about to cross the fence — The Lakshman Rekha. There was no doubt that another Ramayana would happen, in case she was caught by the infamous landlord Desai.

Once in the past, Desai's had detained her at their farm. Mother and I had to bend to our knees to get her majesty released. Landlord had done what anybody on earth would have done in his place — he demanded a penalty as a compensation for the damages done to the crops by Kaali. Thanks to his strangely nonchalant mood that evening, he had satisfied his ego by our prolonged entreaties.

It seemed to me that we were heading towards the same crisis again. Through the gaps of window bars, I could clearly make out that Kaali was sailing close to the wind. Thuppp... teacher flung a piece of chalk at my face with a fierce look. His nostrils expanded in the unison with his brown glary eyes. My right cheek must have had a white blot. The perception of mine, that fluttered here and there like a wild butterfly had come back to a shrewd attention at once and suggested me that 'he is teaching about set theory'.

"Where are you?" he yelled at me with a sharp voice that could even silence the wind.

"Here sir, in cla..." my tongue trailed off for no reason.

"Here? Or at Desai's farm?" he intensified his serious tone.

There followed a pronounced sycophantic laughter. I sought a glance at Swathi by rolling my eyeballs stealthily towards my right; she also must have laughed just the way most of them did, blocking their yellow teeth painted by fluorosis.

"He is looking at his Kaali sir," added Ishwar with the gleeful face.

This time the burst of tittering had propagated till the last row. I was obliged to believe that bad batsmen were good at dragging others through the mud.

"Hey shut up, all keep quiet, silence… silence," ordered the master like a Chief Justice, stroking his thin dry cane to the oak table. It sounded a little synthetic to me — that mannered acting and those feigned eyes.

Meanwhile, Kaali had vanished out of my pace!

"Sir, I will be back in sometime," I exclaimed and ran out of the class to chase my fickling target.

I was forced to imagine the gapes of my comrades during my walk-out like a rebel. Swathi must also had gaped like others chorusing the susurration. My feet were trained to run in any kind of matter concerned with Kaali. By the time I reached, Kaali had managed to devour off the tops of few corn crops at the corner of the field. Any passerby could provide the testimony of her invasion, as white as her milk. I began fidgeting as my legs shaked with wariness and my temples beat up rapider than my heart. My only goal for the moment was to chase her out from the place before the arrival of atrocious Desai. I tended to believe that the pressure sharpens one's focus — I battered Kaali on face randomly with an ad-hoc cane to steer her back towards the small exit gate. On the contrary, she began running towards Desai's shed in the farm. A frame of Desai brandishing his axe, gnashing his teeth to strike at Kaali's glossy hips, flashed in my mind. All of my blood pumped up to the head and I started sweltering ceaselessly. For a split second I cursed the creator for his discrimination towards animals with respect to cognizance. I didn't lose hope as long there was no one around. By and by, I negotiated her will and managed to exit her from another gate towards the east. Before taking a sigh of relief for a second and I had to lope behind that hooligan in the uneven terrain. Soon after crossing the stretch of an empty farm, she jiggled, bumped and went on to sprint as she joined the avenue of a rutted muddy road.

School bell, that rang as though inside my head, tintinnabulated for a while to obstruct the stream of my thought. It compelled me to stop, look back and consider about my satchel which I had desolated earlier in the class. I gave myself a respite by pausing under a neem tree and engrossed in plucking out the grass needles carefully from my trouser bottoms. They looked like the tiny arrows driven into the corpse of a warrior. My feet grew hesitant to turn around as they were apprehensive of one particular thing — what if this vexatious creature enters *payikane*? An open space for defecation with the size of a small playground, surrounded by a head high compound wall, especially built for ladies in the village. Well, of course Kaali was also a lady, but did she go in to defecate? No. It was a perpetual desire of her to scrape her nose to the ground and taste the human waste and at last to take a dip in a morass (her Ganges) which was unused part of the holy *payikane*.

After a brief spell of a deliberation, I got onto my feet to join the muddy road and trudged to follow her way. There was no clue of her all along the passage. No tinkles, nor the grunts. Yes, she did not disappoint me. As I surmised, she had already crossed the main road and had entered the 'zone'.

I held my head high and waited on the patchy tar road, right in front of the wall with PAYIKANE written over it in bold in a white paint. I heard the tinkles of her bell and calm snorts. Nonetheless, couldn't dare to enter the zone as it's prohibited for males and neither could I pelt the stones from over the compound with a wild guess, having no idea of the people inside. I resorted to make some 'cluck cluck' sounds from outside, but of no luck. Buffalos aren't as sensible and sensitive as dogs and humans. I jiggled helplessly and yearned for some action.

Out of nowhere, like a scene from a dream, I happened to recall the lesson of Ekalavya. 'He was the master of archery and an inspiration for every student who genuinely craves to learn anything in this world. An absolute example for a self taught maven. You heard of Shabdhavedhi? He mastered it without a Guru but merely by his Bhakti the devotion. He was the man who could shoot seven arrows at once to the mouth of a barking wild dog, aiming at it just by its sound but not the sight…' peroration of my teacher reverberated in me again like an incantation. Seduced by the anecdote, I picked up a stone (not seven), closed my eyes and aimed my target by the sounds — the tinkles, snorts and her hard grunts. After a brief brood, launched it like a cannon ball, and that's it.

I found my closed eyes pinching the very next moment as I heard a slosh and spill of a plastic pitcher, followed by a coarse "Hey rascal, who is that, don't you have any shame, don't you have any ladies back home? Can't I at-least sit here peacefully? You pushy perisher," from inside. I sprinted back and hid behind a bush near water tank. After few moments or so, the same courteous lady smacked Kaali and chased her out with stones and yells. I waited there in my hiding place till that lady departed, but meanwhile Kaali waded herself into another pond of open sewer beside the zone and dipped in it.

I grew exasperated and muttered "Such an inglorious beast" and then walked out of my temporary hideaway with a lost face.

Avva arrived at the end like the police to a crime scene. We both battered Kaali, till she waded out in the avatar of a muddy statue. Mother took her to nearby stream to get her bathed. I jogged back to school with a last and least hope to get the bag back. But, as I guesstimated, Mr.Diligent peon Rangappa had already locked the doors. I checked if I could play something from the window but they were latched too. For a moment I thought it's a nice alibi to relax at home. But what if there was any homework assigned?

Along with the drowsy sun, I paced bedraggled towards the home. Our 'Gully Gang' a handful of boys, was busy playing carom under the banyan tree, which was a natural umbrella for a line of houses. Adda is what they called for that deck-like stone platform around the massive trunk of that ancient tree. I always thought they hated me for the fact that their parents belabored them by pointing at me as a model child. My orderliness and punctuality to the school and helping mother at home were adverse to the life and style of Gully Gang. Pinto, son of Mariyamma was the gang leader. His mother was a well-known name among gully ladies and gentlemen. She ran a grocery shop and lent small sums of money for interest and her husband Raju had a bicycle cum motorcycle garage. He attended customers only when he was sober.

As I trudged counting my steps by the adda, Pinto threw an inviting smile and beckoned me to play. I crimsoned and replied in reluctance with the hand gesture "I will come back," and hurried forward. Other guys did not notice me much as they seemed to be engrossed in the game. Chennappa was the man who stared at me every day, his Greek-philosopher-like thick beard, untidy attire and a five feet long snake hooded walking stick, certainly scared others but not me. I marched further into the alley crossing the last home of the gully; there you see my home, separate from the gully and so independent, next only to the crumbling veterinary clinic. Kaali slept inside its compound when it rained and also whenever she liked to. Thanks to the massive awning there.

Glossy body of Kaali gleamed in twilight after a stream-bath. Her daughter Dyami was being pulled back from the udder by Avva. She could again drink her share after Mother is done with the milking. Avva patted Kaali's back with water and splashed some to the udder — a regular ritual before milking Kaali. She handed Dyami over to me and began pulling Kaali's teats in an order, one by one in a round robin fashion. I tried to cover Dyami's eyes while Avva was legally cheating her rights and privileges. I too was her partner in crime. Dyami was really a good baby for that matter. Avva named her Dyamavva, as she was born on the day of festival of village-goddess. I called her Dyami. Soon after the bowl was full till its brink, and mother's passion was quenched, I was instructed by mother to leave Dyami out of my clutches as it was her turn to claim her rights, the leftover rights. She sprung out of my hands onto her mother like a magic deer. I was astounded by the magnetic bonding between them. The lights were turned on, to draw a line between the hues of day and the night.

There were around six permanent subscribers to Kaali's dairy — the patrons of compassion. It was my prime duty to deliver the milk to those six houses every evening around seven post meridiem. Before her marriage, Rani agreed to go with me whenever I requested. And there were times when we even shared three houses each. I liked this job of milkman for many reasons. It was like a paid stroll. There used to be exciting events in Bazar Street almost every eve. A spacious stone platform, under a giant mercury vapor light which seemed to derive all the orange from evening sun, was reserved for daily congregations. Like, an assemblage of men gaping at an army officer, while he fervently shared his war-time experiences with spine chilling scenes by his skillful theatric expressions; or few men conferring about the gypsies who lifted the lambs from the herds and so on.

I traversed five houses and for the last home, I had to prepare myself a bit. It's Dr. Revankar's. I entered the gate and waited at the main door. In the hall, Swathi alone was seated on an antique sofa immersed in watching a song played in a black and white TV, ducking down now and then to write something on her notebook with the lost concentration. She struggled and repeated both the actions unvaryingly. As I invaded the aura of the home with "Milk" in a high pitched voice, an impassive look of her reached me in no time. I reciprocated instantly. Time was still for a moment. Mrs.Revankar emerged from the door beside the sofa like an antagonist entering the scene in a folk drama. She grabbed milk bowl hastily and splashed few drops of the milk on to the floor to say, "Oh, here you go, your mother mixes more water as always," and then she swiftly carried the milk inside. Swathi looked at me again, blank with a pretense of studiousness. Mrs.Revankar stormed back with the empty vessel saying, "Ask your mother to give thick milk for doctor's home." I just nodded, as usual and fled the place. It was a daily story, like an eternal mega serial in which my character was reserved only to get the face redden in each episode.

Whenever I was accompanied by Rani, she always forced me alone to go inside, and waited out of the house to eavesdrop and giggle at Mrs.Revankar's repeated words. I remember, one day that I wanted to say that thing to Rani, out of my fury towards this doctor's wife. "Mrs.Revankar deserves today's milk, as Kaali spent most of her day in payikane!" nonetheless, my caginess held my horses back, as it offered me a free advice that it would be like 'spitting towards the sky'. We too at home consumed the same milk. I had a profound doubt that whether Rani would laugh at my joke or my own foolishness. And hence I had buried that idea deep down under the carpet of my memories of being milkman. I made my way towards home pondering on her, did she really like me?

Momentary blue light penetrates through the little gaps of the curtain to remind me of my relation with the existence. The solemn silence floods the room, unperturbed by the play of streaks of faint light. Night falls like her — naked, yet unfathomable.

Chapter 4

"Men find happiness in spying on women than in loving them…"

She had supposed it solemnly, peering down out of the window through the opening of curtain.

Needless to say, that it was a tight slap on my face and certainly on the faces of several such men, who gauge at the shadows of their ladies and invest lives in tracing their spoor.

I had noticed a tall man of wheatish complexion, sporting aviator glasses at the juice bar along the front-road of our condominium, watching over her window like a secret agent. He twitched his shoulders like a wolf between his sour sips.

"Do you know who he is? I have seen him around, watching over your balcony," I had asked her during a lull.

She got up to her feet and paced gently towards me, wrapping up the towel around her milky body with an unperturbed look.

"From how long do you see him around?" she asked, clutching the towel knot above her gainly breast. My shaky hand hurried to open the curtain a little more to accommodate four eyes comfortably; however, her warm hand thwarted the attempt.

"I have seen him from quite some time —" I replied stepping back a little, clasping her tender shoulder.

After a brief pause, "He is the one," she said in an unusually nonchalant stature.

"Your husband?" I enquired naively swallowing up the already scarce saliva. She remained quiet and pensive, staring at him. He seemed to had done with his juice and was holding an empty glass with a castoff straw cleaning off the remnant substance on his smoker lips with his long tongue.

"You said you went through a judicial separation right? What is he doing here?" I asked gathering up a little dry courage.

"Men find happiness in ...."

I closed the curtain furtively and my mind rattled with the burgeoning questions. There seemed a smell of trouble and my feet almost tiptoed towards bathroom chased by wariness. I grow ill at ease in such situations.

"Can you please prepare two cups of coffee?" I called out to her from bathroom. A faint "sure" reached me penetrating the thick door that stood firm between us. I took my own time inside doing nothing, pretending as though I have the necessity to be there, turning the water tap on and off to make some noise with an empty bucket, washing myself and so on.

She was dressed up already by the time I emerged out of my temporary exile. A porcelain cup waited for me on teapoy, wafting up the chaos. We avoided eye contacts. I waited for her to say something and perhaps she too waited, to hear something from me. The silence pervaded the room. Though heard our minds, it refused to concede in anyway — the si-le-nce. Of course, coffee tasted bitter than usual.

Sip by sip, Kaali began to manifest on the canvass of my mind. A milkman drinks coffee without the natural milk — a writer in me was ready to flourish his pen with bunch of ironies to prove himself. I recalled the boy shutting the tender eyes of Dyami while his mother milked Dyami's mother. *Was I too innocent?*

"I can't manage both," I had protested out of an unmeasured annoyance.

"She doesn't harm you anywhere, all that I expect from you is to keep an eye on her, and that's all," mother had declared rolling her scythe up in a piece of cloth, probably a rag cut down from her ancient *saree*, as she got ready for the duty. It seemed sensible on her part. All other affairs like milking, mowing, cleaning the shed and dumping the waste were taken care by mother along with her farm work and household stuff. To 'keep an eye' on Kaali in addition to my school, looked trivial compared to her excruciatingly arduous routine. I was compelled to agree without a second word.

"Hope you all clear with Decimals and Fractions," said teacher Chaitanya, with a fresh temperament to begin the class. Kaali seemed to be in a gladsome mood and grazed by the verges. Desai's gate was also anchored for that day. *If it flows, it flows for a while like the fresh water stream — the life.* I had no fear nor was I sinister. All that I prayed to god was to drive my teacher's mind to forget about the last class incident — my rebel exit from the classroom. I had taken my eyes off from Kaali and gazed at the black board like everyone around, with widened eyes — pretentiously earnest and perceptive.

"Any doubts?" he asked for the third time pressingly, throwing a thrustful look at me. What do you do when you are under a gunpoint? I surrendered.

"Sir, what will be zero divided by zero?" merely for the sake of asking some kind of a doubt, I had asked what sounded to be a valid question that fell in the conformity to the context. I still have no idea of the roots of the impulse that impelled me to ask something like that, which I never contemplated upon.

"Well, a very good question indeed. Anybody, who could enlighten us about this?," he expected someone to answer on his behalf. Nonetheless, all he got was a brief spell of susurration in return. I took a quick glance at Kaali and seemed to grow anxious about the imminent cross questions that could end me up in shambles.

"Well, before looking at zero by zero, can someone let us know what will be ...." He wrote : 0/5 =?, 5/0=? on the black board. A question, part verbal and part visual, had a sort of magic to draw the sharp attention of class.

"Zero by five is zero and five by zero will be infinity sir," said with a croaky voice, the first bencher and the topper of the class, Nilesh.

"So what is infinity?"

"Anything that never ends, sir…" exclaimed again Nilesh in no time.

"Like your nose-run?" asked Chaitanya with an impish wink and the class broke into a wild guffaw. I took a glimpse of Swathi in a twinkle of an eye. She too laughed like everyone else. Nilesh had a never ending stream of snot, like a perennial Himalayan river that flew all through the year. His left hand was always busy in his pocket to fish his glutinous handkerchief.

Teacher opened two mirrors from the drawer and attempted to demonstrate the infinity. "This world is a fusion of finiteness and the infiniteness; it's the very nature of god and his own ultimate expression. This synthesis could be seen everywhere, for example you and your body. Though your body dies, you live forever.

If you step out and lift your heads up, what do you see? The sky. It's boundless, it's infinite, isn't it a miracle? How many of us really think of it?"

He went on to talk about the nature of universe and the soul, the phenomenal and noumenal world and so on. Eventually, the class began to yawn and slacken. Chins were dropped on to the palms and the heads undulated like water lilies. The gravity exerts its force when the mind begins to wobble and vice versa. Chaitanya seemed to have realized that the topic was diverted, like a river changing its course at the slope of a hill. Thus, he concluded the class by inscribing '0/0=?' at the top right corner of the chalkboard and boxed it with a thick rectangle, sacrificing the life of a new chalk-piece. It implied that it's our task to research and find out the answer. I took a sigh of relief as the session ended without causing any ignominy to me.

I was absorbed by a surprise at the lunch-break after witnessing Kaali in a festive mood. There stood a heap of hay under a eucalyptus tree, in the corner of school ground, collected by the students of upper grade as part of a co-curricular activity. Kaali seemed busy devouring it up in excitement. I could unwind in the class peacefully for the rest of the day.

It was teacher Chaitanya who conducted the class again due to the absence of science teacher. Though I fail to ascertain whether this encounter was on the same day or not, I feel comfortable to say that it was the same day. Chaitanya was admired by the entire class for his sense of humor and genial conduct. In my view, it's rare to be austere and approachable at the same time.

"We will see the number series," he proclaimed in a new vigor, displaying his back to the class and began to write a series. The line almost touched the territory of '0/0=?' — the shared eternal quest.

'4, 8, 16, 32, 64, _?' Without further ado, the class echoed by a loud "128 sir…" Mr.Chaitanya must have felt contented with the overwhelming response. Propelled by the vibes, he went ahead to write another series.

'21, 28, 42, 64, _?' A sudden cloud of silence loomed over the class. One looked at the other's face with a question mark on their foreheads.

"Its 91 sir," it was Nilesh again, with the signature croaky voice and the gummy handkerchief in hand at his service, reassured the class of his rank and merit. Mr.Chaitanya looked impressed and uttered, "very good" with an appreciative smile. The class expected an explanation, a glimpse at the play area of Nilesh in his mind; however there was another series about to come. Expect the unexpected.

'200, 165, 148, 117, _?' After a brief mull-over, he announced — "Lucky will answer this time". The sword that was hovering for about sometime finally fell upon me. I stood up firmly and looked at the board for a while; there was no babble this time. "It's 104 sir," I uttered with a strange confidence. Mr.Chaitanya stepped further to take a glance at his notebook on table to confirm himself of the answer. There was an attempted outburst of snigger in the last bench. "Well done!" he said before going on to write a new sequence. There was a big O formed on everyone's face in the class as my eyes surveyed surreptitiously. I held my arms across the chest most of the time to hide my contrast pocket and felt secure in that self-hugging posture. I remained on my feet as if noticing nothing, though I had sought and failed couple of times for a quick glimpse of Swathi. Teacher was ready with another challenge at his disposal, that seemed even trickier — '19, 22, 32, 47, _?' He raked through the class before shifting the attention towards me. The whole grand flock was ducked at once and the pens got busy scribbling and pretending between the fingers. There began the rumblings of papers and pencils as a heat wave of competition passed through the class. An intensity of a running race took over everyone — a sort of a surprise Olympics. On the other end, teacher waited firmly pacing up and down on the stage with a shabby duster in his hand.

Nevertheless, even after minutes, even after an orphan caterpillar drifted its way out of the windowsill, none of them lifted their heads up, including Mr.Runny Nose. (There is a strong suspicion and regret on my moral conscience for my attitude to mock Nilesh for my childhood jealousy towards him, owing to his knowledge and wealthy background to which any girl would look at him unhesitantly.) At last, after a spell of disappointing silence, teacher looked up at me with a nod of approval. "Its 74 sir, and 108 after that." I had brought the race into a halt, to create a class full of question marks again. Teacher uttered "Good" in a confused voice, before the deep clang of school bell that brought all of us a freedom for the day and a new reality. I flumped down to digest and make myself believe what had just happened in the class. I let everyone exit to avoid any possible fuss that my fellow learners could have created around me. I looked at Kaali from the window freely without any constraints or hesitation. She had stretched down as she was done with her mission. Full and contented, unlike humans.

"Lucky..." I heard teacher Chaitanya calling me from the corridor while I was busy taking a turn to left at the end of schoolhouse, so as to approach Kaali with the threadbare satchel on my back. I turned back and jogged towards him with a quirky curiosity.

"Nothing much, had you practiced those series? How could you answer them so quickly?" he asked rubbing his chalk-tainted fingers to one of the textbooks.

"No sir, I haven't. I just guessed and responded with whatever that came to my mind,"

"Well, you can leave. Meet me in staffroom tomorrow." He left, rolling up his sleeves, after my approving nod.

I drove Kaali towards home through the black-soiled naked fields. They all seemed green that day. There was an unknown joy filled in the evening breeze buzzed around me like the song of a blackbird. Colors of the purple sky were descended into my life through the skylight windows of my classroom. Kaali walked calmly as her belly was filled with the benevolence of the children of god.

Every time that I visited this account of my memory, it never failed to perplex me. How plausible was it that I didn't reflect anything while returning home, about the sudden spring of my prodigious prowess in numbers? As I contemplated more and more, I seemed to have got contented with two inferences that complimented each other. In other words, they shaped my armchair philosophy. The first being, in the course of childhood, one merely goes through the situations and experiences, without realizing its magnitude or the implications. No attention is paid towards the cause and effect but all that matters is what happens at the moment. And the second is, whenever anything good occurs, one tends to be drifted into the mood of celebration in no time, as that of an accidental prince. Rarely does he subject the causes to a scrutiny. However, if any bad fate befalls, reasons gain significance like no other and one tends to deliberate much on the means of how it happened.

Mother must have been fervent that evening. I didn't forget to block Dyami's face as avva clasped the thicker teat between folded thumb and rest of the fingers, after a brief splash of waters. Kaali stood calmly the way one sits at the barber shop in complete surrender as though under a spell. There is no clue of what her daughter felt inside in the darkness imposed behind my fingers.

All births are painful but not the conceptions. Even so, it was proved wrong in the case of Dyami. It turned out to be a nightmare for Kaali to conceive Dyami. Why should sowing the seeds also be painful in the world of merciful god? Mother insisted on natural insemination for Kaali after several failures from artificial means. We went in search of a bull, village after village, farm after farm roaming like seasonal nomads. Mother and I had to meander for about ten kilometers to get Kaali pregnant.

That scene is still etched in my mind like a nightmare. The sun had broken fierce that summer afternoon, as we approached a small shed in the middle of a Jowar field. An old man in shorts with the towel wrapped around his scalp advised us to wait under a neem tree.

"He will be coming now," he had rest us assured before disappearing into a thicket of head high Jowar plants. Kaali began to tryout few corncobs strewn along the dyke where we stood. Mother quenched her thirst from a clay pot placed in the shade of a green-bush by the dyke. A giant bull with a glossy bulk, wiggling its ears loomed by the shed. A deep wilderness in him must have aroused, it seemed to be boiling up some sort of a rage. Kaali, whom I had thought the most rough and hard, now looked delicate and fragile compared to the deadly beast. Mother looked extremely concerned and fretted.

'Goddess Dyamavva must save Kaali,' I heard avva murmuring closing her eyes for a second.

A dark and tanned man with curly hair emerged from behind the shed. His massive belly arrived seconds before him. His bullish bulk, yellow teeth and all of other uncouth gaucheries were fortifying the fact that he must be the owner of that monstrous bull. Also he must have been its biological brother in his past life. Soon after asking about our whereabouts, he took hold of Kaali and tethered her up to the trunk of the neem tree. Kaali protested in her limits, this intrusion by an alien. Mother and I were there to convince her to stand brave and straight. The old man in shorts had arrived already and was busy unfastening the rope of the male for the showdown. Kaali began to agitate and tremble. Mother scraped Kaali's forehead and horn base with a stick to keep her steady and compel her overlook whatever she was going through, a sort of anesthesia before the operation.

There was a sudden jerk about Kaali's nature and I turned towards my left to discover that the male had begun the attack with its scintillating pizzle which seemed like a bell from hundred hells ringing at once for Kaali. The guy sniggered for its every rise and miss. Making contact was not too daunting a task but wasn't that easier too. Finally it happened, as if the earth was bisected. Kaali sustained, grunted and looked petrified. Mother had held her heart in hand. Her eyes were welled up but she pretended to look bold and neutral. Kaali behaved a little traumatic for a while. 'It's all strange in the god's creation' — I brooded like a grown up. He had charged sixty rupees, for his animal's semen, the owner of the bull. When mother tried her best to bargain, he had responded in a vain and mischievous tone — "Did you not see how strong he is, a trophy winner in the village fair. Whatever that you have paid is actually nowhere up to his worth."

Dyami had jumped off my clutches on to her mother as my mother was done with milking.

Like a nervous amateur artist, I prepared myself for my character of milkman that was to be played for the evening episode. I combed my hair with fingers and wetted my ever parched lips before entering into Dr.Revankar's house. To my disappointment Swathi wasn't there. The hall looked bleak in her absence, like a moonless sky, like the forehead of a Hindu widow. I loitered there for a while at the door before announcing "Milk..." with a passionate hope for her manifestation. However, the dog's tale, her mother stormed out dashing the dark portiere. As per her tradition she was obliged to speckle few drops on the floor to mutter "It's the same." She barged into the kitchen in a hurry that one would surmise rear-end of the house was set ablaze. Her short exchange relieved me to some extent and I felt a little better for the dog's tale.

I was driven by an impulse to take a different route back to home through Bazar Street. My little adventures never seemed to disillusion me. As I approached towards the Gowri Temple in market square, I met with a strange site. The mercury street-light that used to loom like a giant Christmas beetle was off and obscured in the oblivion and there were many standing silhouettes of crowd swarming against a flickering light on a wall. Impelled by my curiosity, I jogged further towards the scene. Then, I realized that it was a free film being projected on the wall.

They were driving the nail with hammer into the palm of a clumsy man who was already caked with blood. The man was tied on to intersecting beams and was suffering the death. People watched this spectacle with their sympathetic wet eyes and some with wince. As I struggled to fit my head between the shoulders of the people at the fringes to achieve a better view, one of the men who appeared to had arranged the show, called me up to his Omni vehicle which was parked in a dark corner away from the scene. I like the name 'Omni'. He offered me a red book drawn out from a carton box; it had a bookmark of a red thread. I didn't bother much of what's the book about, though the appealing golden embossed title — 'New Testament'. I enjoyed my cake and ambled towards home. The omniscient, omnipotent and omnipresent god was carried in an omni vehicle from village to village. It seemed interesting.

It was after many years that I realized such religious conversion campaigns were rampant during those days, the acts of bamboozling the confused. Another incident that came on my way was when after my graduation I was put up as a paying guest for initial few days of my work. It's during that period that I happened to come across a family of a taciturn caretaker who were influenced by a touring Christian evangelist and were eventually converted. I keenly observed all of their confused religious inclinations. They hung photos and calendars of Jesus on walls and covertly worshipped lord Ganesha. They behaved like the pets that lost their owner. They seemed to be in a never ending whirl of chaos.

Soon after reaching home that night, I must have hurled that book into the fissures of earth behind our shack. I believed it slipped into the bowels of earth as I did not hear any thuds in return. As the village got inebriated with the silence of night, as the clouds pleaded the wind for a hiatus, there was a mild regret dawned in me of missing to catch a glimpse of Swathi. Fragrance of mirabilis and visions of her began to invade my being as I lied awake on my straw mat. I recalled her smile filled with admiration towards me in class. The breeze brought in a song emanating from father's radio from the front yard. Its melody was special than the usual ones, as special as Swathi's smile, a sort of Elysian. It still remains special as it's forgotten, the more I tried to recollect, the more elusive it grew — like the golden deer that enchanted Sita.

Chapter 5

It's the strange light that quivered me up from the deepest slumber. A flaming piece of sun must have bombarded at the doors of my eyes. That was the first time ever that I had experienced such frenzy of blinding light. As though an ascetic from a deep down cave witnessing the light after ages, I found myself on the bed baffled, gazing at the glare in the windows.

She had wide opened the window curtain before slipping out like a sleuth. Sun, in his youth and vigor, had invaded my place like never before. I had a feeling of having gotten nude as I trod towards those bare lurid windows, facing the dazzling and unwonted streaks of sun. I hurtled, wriggled and jumped to draw the curtains, to bring them back to their previous positions, to rest them in their long lasting comfort. The very next moment, I was struck by a forgotten thought and found myself peering out through the gap to steal a glance at the juice bar. As his absence was confirmed, I tiptoed towards the washroom. Tiptoeing for what? I had no idea; it was as instinctive and involuntary as the blink of eye.

I stood in front of the mirror for a while, staring at my person like a stranger whom I met by chance. One is stranger to oneself after a dreamy slumber. That's how I put it. My right eye seemed to be little bloodshot. I must have had rubbed it brutally in sleep. In a flash, a gentle hand of an immediate thought waded me into the murky marsh of memory. I was coerced to recall the most terrifying surreal nightmare that I was forced to sustain. In fact, the gruesome effect of it must be the reason for my sudden jolt-up.

I cannot ascertain on how old I was. I must have had diabetes — a disease of the rich. There were lines of dark ants swarming in the toilet bowl. It seemed that I never paid any heed nor I showed any concern for it. That night, I must have got inebriated or must be terribly drowsy. There was an unprecedented itch in my right eye, a gravely painful paraesthesia with an inescapable irritation. I scraped it with my pointy long nails and must have stabbed and gashed the eyeball. Suddenly, it fell off me like a painted golf ball. I felt a huge cavity in my skull. It must have rolled on the floor and made its way towards some godforsaken corner behind the furniture. I crawled under the fitments and there was no way I spot it. Did it try to spot me? How could it do that without its master? Now, my right orbit hole in the skull began gushing out blood with a new fervor. I struggled to block it with my palm and lost the consciousness in no time.

After hours, I felt soddened everywhere and woke up. I was being treated by a lady doctor, and I strained myself to behold her blurry face through the partially opened left eye. Yet, it was familiar, as familiar as a forgotten favorite song.

"Where's the eyeball?" She asked.

"It's gone, I lost it at my apartment," I replied.

"Well, you want me to sew the eye as is?"

I nodded an approval as I couldn't make out what was going on.

She began sewing it. There was a desire that provoked me to ask 'who are you?', however I was compelled to hold it back with a suspicion. Like a bewildered newborn with the glittering eyes, from the cradle beyond his wriggles and struggles, registering the face of his mother, I gauged at her seraphic smile on that balmy face. When I went on to touch my eyeless hole, she clutched my wrist to forestall the attempt. The song, the same wistful special song, played in the background. It was too faint to discern, it was too vague to put a name to. She rested my hand on my chest with a grace of an angel and said, "I am Swathi," and left the place in a flash. I made my way towards the dazzling door with an impaired vision. All looked hazy and blurry. My father was lying on charpoy, tuning his radio clumsily. He looked up towards me and smiled. At this point, there must be a little convincing clue that suggested 'It should be a dream'. I stirred up.

If there's anything that frightens me the most is a nightmare. It makes me feel primitive, a too bodily and embryonic being. One tends to lose all the control over his life in dreams; he has to go through everything that comes his way without his discretion, like a convicted prisoner, like a slave. One has to get caught without any resistance, if a tiger catches him in its giant chops. Nightmares remind me of sickness, they remind me of death in a terrible manner, especially the afternoon dozes which turned out to be of a macabre nature. Thus, they obliged me to remain wary of naps during day time.

The eyeball-dream has got all the merits to get inscribed very next to the train-dream in the plane of my memory. It is one such dream which I lived as intensely as the reality (if there is any).

The train that I was traveling in had come to a halt in the middle of nowhere. It was a desolate and desert like terrain all around. A sort of a misty moor. They announced that there's no track laid further. I seemed to had an unknown urgency to reach the destination. I got down from the train and began marching towards a thicket in the distance. As soon as I crossed it, I found myself on a muddy road that meandered towards a village. It was lush green all along. There were numerous livestock grazing merrily in the meadows — buffaloes and cows, small and big. I kept my feet busy pacing past them. Some of those beasts paused and stared at me cudding a strange wariness.

As I made my way into the village, expectantly a port of call in my journey, I happened to meet-up with a lady who appeared like a disremembered friend of mine displaying an unusual amiability with me. With a mysterious gait, she walked me to an old cafe and offered some bread and drink. I must have asked her about the path to proceed towards my destination. She aimed her hand towards a tunnel at the end of the village and conjured up a graceful smile.

There were giant vines of lightening flashing in the sky with terrifying thunders. Yet, there wasn't any rain. My throat parched frequently. I ran through the burrow and when I reached the other end, I began to pant bitterly. There was an old jeep perched on a cliff flailing as the people were swarming on to it. Nonetheless, I did not find any road as such. As I paused there perplexed, the thunderstorm hammered with the intensity that sky was broken apart into two halves. The crowd dispersed in a slow motion crying and shrieking to save their lives. Within the blink of an eye, the jeep slipped and fell into the valley as though an invisible monstrous hand pulled it down. I couldn't dare to look into the fissure created in the sky. As my heart seemed to stop any time, I darted back through the tunnel. The ceiling lights in the tunnel flashed at every turn casting kaleidoscopic patterns everywhere. A resonant sound of a gargantuan machinery echoed till the end of it. As soon as I made my way out of the tunnel into the village, it was all calm again. There was no rain, no tumult; a stillness of the desert had pervaded the hamlet.

She gazed at me with a conspiratorial smile from the door of her cafe, but I chose to steer clear of her from my way. There was no option left for me, save for trudging back the way that I had taken before.

Even in the bright sun, I couldn't see at a distance. The journey of unnerving experience continued, as I found that all the lively farm animals manifested earlier had turned into the decaying carcasses now. There were mere flesh and bloody bones strewn all along the path as the vultures swarmed over them. My panic-stricken person jogged towards the thicket as the last resort, to reach the train. Once I crossed it in haste, there was no train to be spotted as such. I found myself in the middle of a never ending desolate plain. A haunting misty moor.

I had no clue on why such a petrifying dream had occurred to me then. It was many moons ago and I never gave it a thought to dissect or comprehend it; neither could I make sense of it now. I am not in favor of those who profess the idea that dreams have got meanings in them. One thing I could assure is that they bring out a mysterious artist in every human being, a befuddled artist with nebulous notions.

I vented to contemplate on what might have triggered this eye ball dream, while I donned my jacket for the stroll. There was no reason found which could appeal me to plough in its direction. My stream of thought took a different course all together at this juncture. It provoked me to deliberate on why I liked Swathi. In other words, a consideration on the rationale behind my fondness towards her. She wasn't of a great complexion like Noor, nor did she possess the great body features like Reshma or Sushmita. She was beautiful for no reason, like a poppy, like the tender smile of an infant, like a dew drop, like the sunset, like the mother-nature

— the god's ultimate expression. Her neck was a little longer like that of a swan's. I had seen her calves under her long skirt on a rare encounter while she was busy playing koko. They looked like the legs of a hen. *In juvenescence we tend to like things for no reasons. We like them for the sake of liking.* I arrived at a conclusion before long.

I sported a cricketer's hat and brown sunglasses — a decent alternative to the outright mask; a proven way of social distancing, which is mainly employed by, as far as I know, the celebrities, criminals and reclusive artists. *What am I now?* I made an effort to eavesdrop at the door from inside to assure myself that there's no one in the passage way. I opened the door on the sly and sneaked towards the stairs to avoid passing by her door. A deep sigh acknowledged my decampment at the end of the descent. Incidentally, I took the second exit as I could dodge the inquisitive eyes of notorious watchman.

Cities are not the same when it rains. The heavy rain had turned into a rhythmic mizzle by the time I alighted at Imperial Street station. I had no thoughts or plans for the moment but to sip the coffee and play the role of a bystander for a while. I essayed to survey on the young women and men passing by, speaking in forced accents, perhaps about some cult western film, or about a book of an author who wrote about cats or about the affair of a television star or about the new episode of a Korean drama and so on.

A small cluster of fervent youth which seemed to be full of joys of the spring, was busy offering free hugs for the strangers who walked their way. It appeared to be a sort of a campaign. A hunger sprouted in a wildest corner of my being after looking at an ebullient, well-endowed lady with a complimentary curly hair.

Like any other stroller I too was obliged to act on spur of the moment and made my way towards the gang. I thought it to be awkward to go and stand before them for a hug just like that; hence, I decided to wear a smile and framed a question as well in my mind to avoid any unforeseen mortification. As I grew closer, a pole that crowned the street lamp stopped me to ask — 'What are you trying to achieve?' It refrained me from proceeding further and I loitered in the lee of it, merely at a distance of few feet from my imagination. What was I trying to achieve? By pressing her bosom against mine? By sniffing at her perfume? I was taken aback by my snatched decision. Do they think they could spring up the love and compassion in the core of alienated humans by a mere hug? Does the happiness propagate with much ease like a modern day disease, by a mere hug? Gradually, I shifted the culpability on to their shoulders and drifted away from that place.

As I approached towards the end of the street and my interest, there was a teen with a hippie prosopography standing on the footpath. He played guitar and sang discordantly in a hoarse voice, seeking attention with a slate placed beside him that read, 'Help me join music school'. Several of them captured his photograph and few donated coins out of reluctant sympathy. I did neither.

A video blogger who arrived from nowhere, paused and asked questions to every stroller — "Are you a virgin?", "When did you lose your virginity?", "Do you think your boyfriend is a virgin?" and so on. Few girls shied away and few who seemed to be high with liquor or hookah answered boldly and even explained boisterously about the encounters in which they lost their maidenhood. My eyes fell on a slender midriff of a lady with a crop top. The last rain drop of the evening that slipped through her cleavage descended and trickled down into the belly button, it must have turned into a pearl. I amused myself as I drifted further through the crowd.

Towards the conclusion of my stroll I was obliged to stop by an old book shop, glancing at the children who tormented their parents for comic books. Few of their appeals were granted and the rest were rejected mercilessly. I grew engrossed gazing at the scene as it provoked me to recall my first encounter with the non-academic books.

That was the first time ever that I had set foot into a place of the sort of a staff room. Up till then, it remained a myth for an outlandish student like me. Nilesh and Ishwar had its generous access for fetching the maps and the globes to the class, however I had never got a chance, perhaps I never desired one. It was a large and brightly lit decent room with a huge oval shaped conference table in the middle, covered with a green cloth — a signature of government institutions in our country. The walls were strewn with political maps, lists of the names of all the headmasters who served there since the inception of school along with their tenure; names of the politicians who sanctioned funds for new buildings and also the names of the current members of school development and monitoring committee and so on.

Many a times, I deliberated about the ideas and motives behind the notion of inscribing these lists of names. The way presidents and prime ministers enjoy seeing their names engraved on inaugural plaques, our teachers and clerks also seem to believe that they too are becoming the part of the history — rivets in the chain of legacy (in their limits) by having their names written over such obscure walls which are witnessed by no one but themselves.

"Engineers build the nation, Doctors protect the nation, Commanders defend the nation and the teachers are the ones who create all those men" — Swathi had delivered a convincing speech on teachers' day with an intensity that each of these words were surely sunk into the breasts of every audience and had resulted into a huge applause. Each of the audience at the end of the speech seemed to have agreed upon one common fact that 'teachers deserve more'. Thus, teachers and clerks too are the vital parts of the history, not merely the kings and commanders.

There were few privileged girls of higher grade gathered already at the other side of the table. I thought girls are always privileged in some or the other ways. He acknowledged my entry with a look that carried a sort of affection and warmth. Girls were busy leafing through an old Encyclopedia. Teacher Chaitanya made me sit on the wooden chair opposite to him and surprised me with few more problems concerned with number series and instructed me to write the answers in his notebook. I wrote one by one as quickly as I could.

"Now tell me, how do you get these answers so swiftly and miraculously?" he asked looking into my eyes with veneration.

"There's nothing about it sir, even I have got no idea, and they just appear on my mind like the rainbows in the sky."

Though it sounds a cliché, that's how I had replied my teacher — 'they appear on my mind like the rainbows in the sky'. A gaze of him directed right into my eyes seemed to seek the access to a little more depth of my mind. After a brief dialogue, he broached the topic of my daily plight and insisted that he would talk to my mother in regards to the matter of Kaali. He wanted me to study well, which apparently meant that he never wanted me to waste my life chasing a frenzy buffalo. I pleaded him to let it go, for the matter that avva couldn't take Kaali along with her to the lush green farms where she worked, as those were too delicate for Kaali's nature. "You are free to choose any books from the library and you can even carry them home," he assured releasing his stare from me, straightening up the sagged newspaper in his hands. I must have looked bewildered.

"The first almirah is full of mathematics and science books," he said pointing towards an old cupboard with rusty hinges and glass doors tainted here and there with blue paint.

"The other one contains some old history books which I think are not ripe yet for your interest."

Though I liked books, couldn't form a concrete answer for a reply. I stepped towards the first case and began surveying about the titles on spines through the faded glass doors.

Teacher Chaitanya was back to his reading. I had a deep suspicion on whether he asked me to read more or there's a hidden agenda sketching up to assign an extra homework to me. I was undoubtedly at a loss. The girls lifted their heads up and peered at me and then ducked back, like a bunch of hasty sunflowers. They must have found me amusing.

"Don't hesitate to open it and pick the one that interests you," he said with a smile of approval, looking over from his shoulder. How could I know what interests me? I was not used to be choosy; I never had a luxury of it. I plucked out two books, chose them for their tiny size. One was about Shakunthala Devi's number theory and the other one a brief biography of Srinivasa Ramanujan. I quickly strolled through the pages of the books and found a small portrait of Ramanujan placed safely inside the biography. I took it out to have a glimpse in close-up.

"You can take them home; don't just fritter your time away. A day without reading is a day wasted." He was transformed into a class teacher from a friend-like-being, in the matter of few odd breathes.

I thanked him awkwardly and directed my squinted gaze towards Desai's farm through the massive windows of staff room. Kaali was in her limits, well away from her *Laxman Rekha* which she was not supposed to cross. As and when, Rangappa rang the bell, all the girls rushed out throwing inquisitive smiles at me, to their classroom to grab their bags and set themselves free.

I humbly loitered about Chaitanya, as he was busy keeping his lunchbox back to his bag. Finally, he took out his jacket to wear and paused at it to say, "What are you waiting for? You can carry those books with you. Will you go with me till the water tank near your home?" How could he ask such a thing despite being well informed about Kaali? I replied with "Bye sir…" and left the place to see about Kaali.

My tryst with mathematics had budded that day.

The lights were turned on subliminally. Infant clouds of the gloaming were struggling to prove their loyalty to the wind. Earth strived hard to prove its fertility. Somewhere, the flowers fought hard to preserve the fragrance in their wombs for the unknown tomorrow. The life was on an endless swing, mine and yours.

Chapter 6

Whenever father looked fretful, mother used to taunt him with a remark: 'Why do you behave like a cat whose tail is burnt?' Literally, that's how I seemed to behave, like a cat with his tail burnt. After the episode of spy, I chose to remain distant from her presence both physical and psychological. I ignored checking her messages deliberately and piled them overdue for the responses. To avoid the confrontation with her menacing eyes in the premises, I obliged myself to reach my room late in the night, and to leave early in the morning; repeated this newly conceived habit with the sincerity of the suns and the moons. As for the weekends, I chased myself out with some or the other cerebral engagements pertaining to the recollection of the memories from the remote past with a hope to fill up an empty page or to renovate an image in the mind.

I don't deny that she too had ceased to send messages after a while. My secretive gaits in the apartment corridors and furtive movements must have compelled her to comprehend the underlying reason. She must have derided and even had a laugh at my cowardice. As for me, it's not an act of coward but of a wise. It's a desirable trait of a wise man to keep himself away from the imminent dangers.

As the clouds veiled the blue of the sky, as the shadows swallowed up the light, an aura of gloom hung around me. What seemed to bother me the most was, her silence. It's true to some extent that the silence resolves issues, but I suppose it is only at the cost of a risk of creating more. The strange quietude and pretense of passivity of the nations during the Cold War, stood the world on its toes for decades and the same silence could have ended up the planet earth into an irreparable state — I brooded. There were no signs of any attempts from her end to contact me. At times I did think that it's good for me to dismiss her thoughts like a deciduous tree that sheds its leaves for the season. However, my other mind poked me with an inkling that almost whispered in my inner ears — 'something must be fishy'. I continued my skulking days anyways.

My self-imposed lonely strolls never failed to lift me up from a claustrophobic frame of mind and induce me with jolly moods though transient in nature.

I believe, coffee shops are invented to construct and construe the relationships. Ideas and alliances born and die there like the tides of a full moon. Cafes create a certain soiree mood and offer you a sense of association with the existence. Every sip of coffee that you gulp reiterates the fact that, you aren't alone in the ship.

I don't think that people choose coffee shops for privacy. If that was the case, they would be contented with parks or movies. Coffee is the base on which they build their castles and mansions, that float and stand, that drown and rise. They appear to yearn for the lively background stories; they can't see each other in the eyes for a longer time; and hence they hanker for something sparkling around, to fill up the awkward silences and embarrassing pauses. Even when they are two, they both feel lonely in seclusion. They want to immerse themselves in the fashions and trends of the generation, to feel comfortable in the arms of the society and homely with the life.

Well, for me alone, coffee shops are like refugee camps.

I pondered.

A wary tricenarian gentleman in the corner — that's how people must have referred to me in case I was touched-on anywhere in their conversations. I surveyed all the faces in the cafe, one table after the other to make sure that they are all strangers. With every mouthful of a *café-latte*, I seemed to grow more vigilant, especially when I happened to come across anyone sported with aviator glasses or the long hair. One sees whatever he wants to see. Everyone begin to look like the one whom you have in the mind, the fear clones, that's what I call them.

Beyond the table of a bashful couple, I absorbed myself in gazing at the fountains in the front-yard of the coffee shop through the glass walls. My eyes strained to penetrate the thin flying haze created by the sprinklers, to grasp the images beyond. They were ladies clutching the tender hands of their children employing an extra solicitude, pausing for an opportunity to cross the road. Now, there was a hint of suspicion that my café-latte is merely an alibi to escape my own childhood that I have begun to relive.

Past is something that you think you can chase, only until you realize that you are being chased by it.

My theatric mind ventured to reflect metaphorically that the coffee is my present life and the milk my childhood. Bitterness or the blandness neither could be tasted exclusively, when the god buys you a café-latte — I jotted down.

As I zoomed my gaze out and shifted the focus from the main road to the glass walls, I saw myself reflecting there. I saw myself sitting on the pillion of teacher Chaitanya's moped, and riding on the meandering roads with the backdrop of red skies and a little larger sun.

"See lucky, what I feel is, no matter how random we produce a sequence, there is always a pattern in it. The capabilities of our mind could only produce the numbers that fall into a certain pattern, the reason being, our mind and this whole existence itself is based on a pattern.

An apple seed can produce only apples and an apple can produce only apple seeds, not of the mango or guava. Everything in nature has got the capability only to create its own clone with the similar essence. It's the same with our minds; all that we express is a mere expression of its own orderly aspects.

When we grow conscious of patterns, we crave for the randomness and when we are hounded by the randomness of our life, we seek pattern in it.

Whenever a scene prolongs or repeats in a film, you feel bored, and also when a sequence of numerous different shots played in front of you in a short span of time, you tend to grow agitated, isn't it? It's hard to digest either of them. There is a tempo that life follows, there is a rate your heart beats with, there is a rhythm that the nature functions in, that is what we seek in everything. And it's the same case with numbers."

He offered me a little breathing space, perhaps to let me assimilate all that he said. However, the charged wind that we drove through, swallowed up most of his words.

"Are you sitting well?"

"Yes sir,"

"Listen, about your case, I should tell you something. There's an interesting word called intuition, which means, without any intervention of our logical mind, our consciousness manifests directly in the form of answers. This existence blesses very few with such a rare talent, somewhere an Einstein and sometime a

Ramanujan in the spatiotemporal continuum. The secret behind their extraordinary works is that they never cluttered their mind but allowed the nature to express its mysteries through them. They were merely the vehicles of nature's ultimate wisdom and that is the reason that their works look other worldly to us. There was a great painter who painted the stars as spirals, more than a hundred years ago from now. Who do you think gave him the idea to do it that way? No one but stars themselves. They wanted to photograph themselves through his soul. They wanted to express their true quiddities through him. He was a mere vehicle. He was a chosen. God has blessed you with something precious of that sort. The magic door of intuition is ready open for you. The greatest of the artists, scientists, philosophers and the yogis go through a great penance merely to witness the streaks of light seeping out through the small gaps and holes of that door, now and then. But you are born with the door wide open. You are a chosen. Now, it all depends upon how you nurture it and how you utilize it best for the betterment of humanity. I agree that, it's hard to retain the mind sanctified and uninfluenced forever in our times, but it's not impossible."

I can't establish that all the words that he uttered made it through my rudimentary mind, but I could discern whatever that he attempted to convey that gloaming.

"All you crave for at the moment is to get down from the bike and go home, isn't it? Laxman?"

He had a laugh with those parched lips before pulling over near the water tank, from where I was supposed to walk till my home. I grew bashful and replied modestly with an incomplete giggle, "Nothing like that sir."

I had got a day off from Kaali as mother did not get any assignments that day. Regardless, I had to be home by the evening for job of a milkman bestowed upon me. As I walked near the Baniyan tree, I observed that the adda looked deserted like never before. Even, the troublemaker and the cane bearer Chennappa was also not seen around. I managed to snitch up his number chart from his ever-made bed by the wooden pole in the *pyol* of the abandoned *Chawadi* and paced towards my home in a suppressed triumph. Mother was ready with the milk, mixed through a comparatively less water than other milk sellers in the village. She seemed to abide by the principle of 'the bad is always better than the worse'.

I strolled with an added enthusiasm and felt as though my feet had got springs fixed. It seems that the further exhilaration was a result of the fact that it was a collection day. I could tip myself a rupee or two from the earnings. As usual, my interest and delight of the evening used to be in those few moments of happening experiences in Dr.Revankar's house.

I sneaked into the abode and stood inside the door with a conscientious stature. My breath was held captive before I called out, "Milk…". Swathi looked engrossed in her routine — toggling her gaze between television and her king-size notebook; she had combed her glossy hair and had smeared three horizontal bars of holy ash on her generous forehead, an expected look to be worn before beginning the studies. Right above her, on the wall hung a portrait of Basavanna who also wore the holy ash on his forehead, with a quote written down below at his chest — 'Work is worship'. Beside Basavanna, there were many other portraits of *vibhuti* bearers who should be Swathi's ancestors. A common bulb of a strawberry shape, flickered and spilled its red streaks over all of those frames.

There seemed a duet song playing in the television, *beladingalaagi baa, thangaaliyaagi naanu, aanandava needuve, ondaaguve....* Come to me as the moonlight, and I shall become the breeze, to please you, to become one with you...

Before she could think of becoming the moonlight, she shifted her gaze towards me and paused her eye lashes. I reciprocated. It must have looked like an eternal mute communication between the celestial bodies with a common center, during their perigees and apogees. As for the exception of that evening, she conjured up a smile at me and I was about to acknowledge with all the vehemence, however...

"Oh, you are here, I didn't hear you calling," her mother stormed out dashing the curtain of the door as anticipated.

I took a step back and gave her enough space to splash few drops i.e. her daily ritual to testify her own skills and my mother's ethics. I was swept by the surprise that she did not speckle any drops. By grabbing the jar of milk in haste she scooted her way towards the kitchen, stopped at the door and turned over mysteriously like a social wolf, only to ask, "How much for this week?"

"Hundred and forty six madam," I replied instantly. She disappeared behind the swaying portiere. The song went on in television — *beladingalaagi baa, tangaaliyaagi naanu...* Swathi looked mindful and I dared to gawk at her. Like a filmy soap bubble, her smile reached me leisurely and got busted on my face to liberate all the pressure it wombed through its way. I seized the opportunity to acknowledge this time. The song continued.

"Is it including the balance of four rupees from last week?"

"Yes madam,"

"Oh well, you seem to be very intelligent in calculation. In the same manner, why can't you also display your intelligence in asking your mother to serve a little thicker milk to Doctor's house?"

I received the empty jar with the money and stepped out with a crimsoned face. I overheard Swathi suggesting to her mother, "He is the topper of our class in maths,"

"Oh really, what the hell are you doing with this t.v then? Don't you have any shame being a daughter of doctor, praising scums like him for their talent? Why can't you do it yourself? What is lacking? Are we not providing you with all the best of privileges?"

The song had stopped abruptly. I walked away to drift from darker to the darkest corner of the street. Things had changed at least for the slightest of the precision in the case of the dog's tale. She did not sprinkle the milk on floor.

In the matter of few moments, I found myself gazing at the stars, standing outside my home. They twinkled with the ever new glitter. At times, they looked like the rubies and emeralds placed for exhibition by the god. My eyes seemed to sharpen their gauge — 'Are they spirals?'

I did not vent into any adventures with respect to experimenting the routes back to home, since the chart that I had brought home from the adda was waiting for me. It had aroused my curiosity from many days. A table of two digit numbers with last few boxes left empty to be filled, like the last few candles waiting to be lit. My pen urged me to employ it, like the arrow that pleaded Karna to shoot it against Arjuna. I filled up those boxes in a strange impulse. The same pen of mine felt complacent with the pride of completing the life of that table, as though like a man offering a married life to an orphan widow.

I had a great deal of idea about this game for its prevalence in the milieu. It is called *matka*. They draw a number anything between 01 to 99. Whoever succeeds in guessing the right number, wins eighty times the amount of their bet. You get the mountain or you lose the rope. Naturally, most of them in our village were ready to stake the rope for a mountain of fantasy, and they had turned into chronic, lifetime gamblers. Most of them carried these crumpled charts in their pockets like an inevitable asset. 'Last year's first Monday of the third month was 13, so tomorrow is the third Monday and it will be 31'; 'It was 65 four days ago. So add 4 to it, it becomes 69 and then add the digits. It becomes 15, and that's what will be the number today' — These were the sorts of deliberations and notions, I heard over the period of time, in different places, precisely at the addas like Baniyan tree, Babu's hair saloon, water tank, the mercury light platform and tea stalls in the Bazar Street and so on. Hundreds of such logics were in the currency. All the atheist gamblers, who resorted to the 'luck of logic' had derived their own formulae, as unique as their thumb impressions. I had heard of a man from village nearby, who had made fortune with it and several who had sold out all of their possessions in the pursuit of right numbers. There were men who had fled to Goa chased by the creditors, and the men who never returned. I had seen similar charts in father's pocket as well, when he left his shirt on charpoy as elegantly as a snake that leaves its skin, in his inebriated state, but I had folded and placed it back like a good son then.

The very thought of this game held the wide-eyed country boy awestruck. *How ridiculous is it that the numbers change someone's fate? How absurd is it that one man makes decision on how a community should lead their life?* People of my village, gambled with the rain and when they were lost, they gambled with numbers and when they were lost they gambled with the life. How preposterous. I wanted to scream aloud and break the silence of the night, I didn't. But the rage against gambling boiled me even in the cold night.

Father's radio was slept as serenely as its master. Amidst the grunts and snorts and snores and chirps, it was silence that chorused the silence.

It is almost the witching hour. Ghosts must be having their jamboree somewhere. I have begun to suspect that I am growing insomniac. I open the balcony door and freeze myself in the chilling breeze. Circumstantially, I get possessed by a strange pity on a lonely sock that hangs at the end of clothesline. Its partner is taken away by the rainstorm. It is no longer mine; perhaps it is no longer anyone's. It is abandoned. It would refuge in a dark corner if I rescue it. That flimsy clip, how long can it hold the stray in its arms? (Or the clutches?). And, that's how I dissolve into the night, discovering the miracle in mundane; waiting for the blue light concealed in the breast of night sky.

Chapter 7

Rises and falls of my stocks, do not impact my pulse anymore. Nevertheless, I follow the financials of those patron companies to some extent. I suppose I have fathomed out that like the tides in the sea, the fluctuation is the fundamental nature of a share market. At any point of time, I can retire by merely pressing the sell button. That's what my mind boasts of. All the wealth that I created so far is virtual, like a long distance relationship with a telephone girlfriend. It's merely an idea in the mind, an idea of love and possession, a mere idea till I give it a shape by effectuating it.

I write from thirteenth floor, seated in my company library. Other than my life in the apartment and strolls to coffee shops, I dwell in here, in the library, in the nerve centre where the collective consciousness of humanity is preserved. Many believe thirteen is an inauspicious number, but I like this place the most, quiet like a Buddhist cave in the air. Every time I visit here, I get compelled to appreciate its architect for his aesthetic sensibilities; he has designed the windows which look like that of an airplane. My seat is always at the corner as it's close to the coffee machine.

Amidst the mild rustles and susurration, which are merely the pauses of silence, I grow meditative upon my life. *In the temples, churches and mosques gods born and die, but in the libraries they grow and evolve. Silence is the only offering that one could offer to the god and silence is his ultimate celebration.* I choose library over canteen in the breaks, and I choose breaks over my work. Once in a while my conscience sits opposite to me, and asks, "All these years you have been beating a dead horse, aren't you?" I dread and grow serious, and to escape the effect of my rattling, I look out the window — enormous clouds, like a series of white cottony elephants and rabbits go on procession there. I feel one among them, soothing someone's mind and wetting someone's heart. I feel one with the eternal motion of the existence. I offer myself.

"If there's anything constant in this world, it's only the change. Now, I am going to talk about how well any financial organization could acclimatize with the changes and stand strong. Let there be wars, pandemics, strategic foreign policy issues, tariffs, sanctions, import duties, recessions or be it anything. Against all the odds, we still can run our corporation BAU, only if we adapt to this brand new agility model…" — this is the proem I begin my presentation with, from past ten years. I know it's mediocre. The audiences gape at me in awe in the beginning of the session, and they sink and withdraw their faces, towards the end of it. With a guilt of ruining someone's Thursday morning, I step out and never to be seen again for the next six months. They entitle me as an agility master and I have got a yellow badge with 'Champion of Change and Sustainability' written over it. Every employee in my company must have seen me at least once, as this presentation of mine is disseminated at organizational level. In a nutshell, I am paid for selling superficial and theoretical ideas which could never be implemented for their complexities, inconsistencies and inadaptability. Yet they should exist in every modern organization, like an artist in the parliament. All theories remain new and young forever. Despite graduating from one of the premier educational institutions in the country, this is what I do. This is what most of them do — selling the cosmetic modus operandi for a business. I conduct exams on the topic, unlike god I provide the answers as well. I send them all emails with ravishing certificates as a solatium for my peccadillo with their Thursday mornings. I achieve the targets in time and hailed by my colleagues as 'unicorn of the team'. That is how a dark horse attains a mask and a horn of a unicorn.

"If you don't write your own story, you will be a character in others', never become that," he had said it profoundly. The wind blew with a self-assumed freedom, as there were no adversities on its way. Champaign belt is what they call for our region, for its vast expanse of aridness. I call it a bleak and barren moor. Only those are rich who have the access to water and only those have the access to water who are rich. Lives are tossed into the hot sky by this paradox. The central government had planned for a thermal power plant nearby and someday the work will begin on that regard. What else that belt is good for? We have Veena river flowing nearby, but what's the use unless you have canals to channelize it to the thirsty patches of the earth?

We went to an old park near railway station. It looked antique with rusty railings. A creeper had entwined the gate so forcefully that one had to subject his muscle power for a test to open it. Its hinges were crumbling, and the filigree disfigured. *Even the iron decays into dust by the sands of time.* Before my mind could slip into the annihilation by the thought of gate, he began voluntarily —

"As you already know, I have got transfer to Mysore. It's a well thought decision. It helps me pursue my further academic interests. You are one of the rare students I came across, a raw diamond. There's something that you have got, which is invaluable. You must continue your practice and keep the flame alive; your passion for mathematics should never flicker. It will take you places for sure. All you should do is, be watchful, be on guard always, never get influenced; never get sucked into the frivolous affairs of your home and the community."

He spoke rotating up and down a rusty nut into a bolt which he had picked up from the bench. It must be an orphan spare, casted away from the railway track beside. A freight train, which I surmised a coal carrier, creaked and passed by, exhaling a dark cloud of smoke that made interesting patterns above the hazy blue hills. The man in white in the caboose took a glance at us as he faded away with a green flag in his hand. I am always fascinated towards his strange solitary life; though on the rattling wheels but at utmost peace.

"I know, even if you leave math, it won't leave you. Here you go, take this cover; it contains enough money for your next year's admission fees and books as well. I am aware of your financial condition, don't be intimidated by it. All will be fine if we are strong enough to make things fine."

He held an envelope forward — open-end, sealed and folded. As I displayed reluctance to accept, he slipped it into my pocket forcefully. Few boys raced with their bicycles on the parallel road to the rail track. Huge lorries along the horizon, that were destined to Mumbai (that's what we believed) looked like toys of god.

"You can buy a new uniform shirt as well in it." His fingers felt my embroidered pocket for a moment. There was a crinkle under his right eye as he smiled. I didn't know how to react. *Am I too rude and unsocial? To bid farewell to the dearest teacher without even shedding four beads of tears? And a 'thank you' of gratitude?* I despised myself for not being like others.

My memory of how I made my way towards home that evening is as hazy as the blue hills near our village. He must have dropped me till water tank? Perhaps I took a *Tonga* along with train passengers. Nonetheless, there was something dramatic happened before reaching home. I paused by an old *godown*, now a free home for squirrels, and relieved myself wetting a corner, perhaps the roof of a burrow carved by bandicoots, beside that abandoned architecture. And post the ritual, I quickly covered the damp area with the dust. I had inculcated a habit of burying my guilt then and there, like British. An unknown fervor urged me to open the envelope and feel the notes, and even count them if the time permits. I took a quick glance at the surroundings and went ahead to fish out the cover from my pocket to begin, however, a man with an axe on his shoulder emerged out of a bush to turn me dumbfounded. I slid the cover through my satchel in rush and walked away. He departed overlooking my presence, just the way anyone else would have done in his bedraggled condition.

As I darted and advanced towards the adda, the gang was found busy playing carom.

"Hey lucky come over here," it was Pinto who could call me like that. He had a dialect of his own, cultivated out of his Goan upbringing and extensively exploited *gutkha* habit. It seemed, he and his parents were in Goa for many years and had returned recently to settle back in hometown. To have their bodies die and decay in the soil they were born. I progressed forward to ask,

"What?"

"Come here, we need one more chap to play, we are only three," he invited me pointing to the empty seat. The pawns were arranged around the pink-queen in an attractive pattern like a *rangoli* and the striker slid on the powdery board, ready to push the wooden-disks to their fates. I gave in to my temptation for the game and strode towards them with all the confidence that was brewed instantly.

"Let's play a game or two till Monya arrives," he said spitting the *gutkha* to the trunk of banyan tree painting it red.

I took the vacant seat cradling my school bag on my laps prudently.

"Yours are black," he suggested, I nodded.

There was another guy Sunil, who was engrossed in playing some sort of a game in a device. That was the period, when the devices were arrived freshly all the way from China. I was puzzled of how could they get hold of an other-worldly gadget just like that. Pinto took the strike and managed to pocket three pawns in a row. I played average, in fact below average. All that was expected from me was to place the coins near their destiny holes and that's all. Pinto needed a partner for namesake to run the doubles game is what I felt. Beerya, one of my opponents in the game looked at me gingerly cudding *gutkha*, wiping frequently the cracks at the corners of his mouth.

There were few younger boys swarming about Sunil, vying for a place next to him for the better view of the screen.

"What game are you playing Sunya?" asked Pinto scratching his young curly pliant beard, and it turned white by the caress of his powder-ridden fingers.

"Bounce Ball," replied Sunil absent-mindedly, after a considerable amount of time.

"That's all you know?"

"Well no, I know Sudoku as well"

"Give it to me here; Lucky will nail it. I heard he is good at mathematics."

I couldn't believe I would be holding a device in my hands then. Pinto launched Sudoku and handed it over to me. I felt it little heavy in my hand, the device. Mounesh, who had arrived and loitering behind me, took my place in carom. He was the man who guessed the *matka-numbers* and generously disbursed free advice to all at the adda. People believed in his words though his wild guesses never seemed to bear fruit. His elder brothers had gained significant popularity for making entrancing Ganesha idols with red-clay; they seemed to export them to many villages around. Mounesh, was a square-peg in a round-hole in their family. By repudiating the pursuit of his clan, he dwelled out until the end of time in the company, in the hangover, in the game, floating like a feather.

I sat down beside Pinto playing Sudoku and watching how they played carom. Two tasks at a time like Swathi. I tried my best to place the numbers in rows and columns to complete it. It appears to me that I finished it once and was playing second round. Avva presented herself in a distance to remind me of my crown of milkman. "I have got to go…" said I, rising up, handing the device over to Pinto. "Oh why, keep it with you for the night, have fun, return it tomorrow, no issues at all," he insisted. I slid it safely into my satchel.

Many lips and throats would be waiting for my service, for the evening coffee. That's how I carved out my importance in the village. *There's no one important on earth till the essence of importance is apprehended. I am grown up; people have begun considering me as a serious boy and handing over precious gadgets to keep for a night.* For a moment, I touched below my nose to substantiate, and there protruded some bristles but not firm, hence they weren't the real moustache like Pinto's yet? I wasn't sure. I walked briskly to complete my rounding for the consumers' houses and avoided Mudal Street for the fear of a ferocious dog that could change our looks and fates. Its recent encounter was a hot topic in the adda.

All I had in mind was the thought to get back to home as soon as possible. An envelope pregnant with cash and a dreamy gadget to play Sudoku with, waited for me, to push the moon behind the clouds for the night. Course of my life had met with an unbelievable luxury. The cherry on top of the cake was Swathi's unforgettable smile. A visiting preacher from an unknown town prior to the yearly village fair, in his evening congregations, always used to iterate one thing, "Wait for it, oh my children of god wait for it. He will surely bless you, he will surely give you, if he begins to give, your hands are small to receive, and your homes are small to contain his boons. Wait for it." I had come to realize what he actually meant.

The deep hammering sounds of my mother's jowar-roti recipe welcomed me as I emerged in the front-yard. Though the moment was ripe, I did not open the envelope, rather hid it between the pages of my science textbook, next to the pressed dry-leaf of hibiscus. After the supper, I lay awake on straw-mat and began to play Sudoku under the holey blanket.

By and by, the numbers had become an integral part of my life. The dogs barked, frogs croaked, Kaali and Dyami snorted, breeze brought in the fragrance of mirabilis through the holes of bamboo walls of my home. I was so absorbed that all these phenomena seemed to happen at the lower strata of my consciousness. Father did not play any songs that night nor did he sing, he must have reached late and stretched silently on the charpoy. The game went on till the charge was almost empty and the vigor was exhausted. I must have completed it several times in the advanced difficulty levels. Slumber had encroached me like a silent flood that swallows up a village in the darkness. *Men can resist anything, but the sleep,* thought for myself and drifted into the nothingness.

*****

There were streaks of golden light piercing through the bamboo walls in the morning, falling on my face to invite me for the enigmas of the new day. I woke up much late than the sun and even later than my usual timing. There was a mild headache that wobbled me inside the skull, and I felt a little peckish too. With a slight jolt of realization, the first and foremost thing that I looked for was the device. It's natural that one looks for something in the morning that he slept with and immersed with, be it a partner, or a book or a device. Mother was busy sweeping the wet waste of the cattle to dump it to gobar-yard. We sold it when the heap of manure grew equal to the size of a tractor trolley. People bought it to fertilize their fields; a full trolley for a gunny sack of jowar. Precisely, they drank and ate Kaali's organic products all through.

"Avva, have you kept the device aside?" I asked rubbing my eyes, and adjusting my shorts.

"I have not seen any device, what sort of?" she lifted herself the bamboo container to perch it over her head and walked away groaning. There was no clue of father at home. I rummaged through the room lifting up my blanket and the crumbling mat. The dust particles that hung in the air stirred and twinkled bathing in the golden shafts of sun. My legs began palpitating and the throat dried up. I hesitated to swallow the dirty saliva.

Two shadows manifested on the floor from the main door; a taller and a dwarf — Pinto and Beerya.

"Oh you woke up at the right time, pass on the device here, we need to charge it and take it to the town to return it today," he ordered spitting his *ghutka* over the mirabilis. I felt a deep choke inside.

"Yeah ok, let me search it. Actually I don't see it," I was disarrayed, acted, failed and shrugged.

One grinned and the other laughed, I don't remember who did what.

"What do you mean by you don't see it? Have you any idea of its worth? Please make it fast, we need to hurry."

They both stepped further and entered home. I got blacked out and held myself from collapsing. They took the envelope from my school bag in a cold composure and left home with a sense of triumph.

"Your father must have sold it by now, to play *matka*, go check with him," Beerya shouted haughtily, wiping his cracks at the corners of mouth with a last spit on mirabilis, from outside before crossing the frame of door. Mother was back, and everything was normal around me in minutes. The leaves and the buds of mirabilis were soaked red in their *gutkha* spittle. They swayed and dribbled.

I was numb, timorous and the steps were heavy as I walked into the desiccated fields for toilet. I squatted down behind a mound. I wasn't matured enough to analyze and brood on the jolt that I had experienced moments ago, but was drowned into a consequent giddiness owing to the somersault of life. Tears trinkled down into the water in pitcher and created small ripples, measuring the bad times. That was the first instance of crying etched in my mind. I felt lonely and dejected. It were an expanse of dusk lands everywhere around. Sun beated his best. Every word of teacher's advice, I had tossed into the air. Someone used to say, 'Dog belongs to a dog's place'. It suited me so well.

Who would have thought that the events would turn out like this? Shadow of mine defended as I dawdled back towards home.

Chapter 8

Grey mornings seem to aggravate the gloom and the hot afternoons transform that gloom into agony. I hesitated to lay my elbow on the window ledge while seated, as I felt that I lost that privilege and freedom in the class. I was taken over by a sense of alienation and was bludgeoned by an old feeling of outlandishness. Laxman Chalavadi, a name for namesake, for the records' sake, the same old unknown boy whose presence or the absence went unnoticed, had got himself buried deep down again into the fissures of the earth. Teacher Chaitanya's spell in my life was like an afternoon rain. I went blind before could I witness the rainbows — my pen enticed me to scribble the line on the last page of maths notebook. I stepped back mentally and ceased to participate in the class, ducked and eventually withdrawn. It seemed to be social studies class. Mere smile of Swathi could never be a panacea for my grief. With the shyness of a snail I wriggled and scribbled on an already filled up page, as the mind was frizzled by severe anguish.

Loud words of teacher could not make any sort of a difference to my involuntary vow. Teacher Sheshappa — an orthodox moody old-man with an austere pretense, whose name in Kannada meant, 'father of the remains', went on to ask even more loudly,

"Tell me, why do we watch India versus Pakistan matches with an extra interest and feel so concerned compared to the matches with different countries?" he continued after a breathing pause, "it implies that there is a patriot in each one of us. There is a soldier in each of us. Since we are all civilized, we release our aggression through the games instead of wars. It is always safe to play with bats and balls than bombs, isn't it? You know how the wars kick off? Any idea on LOC in the border? The line of cross? Well it is a fence in the frontier. Neither the Pakistanis nor the Indians should cross it. You know what happens if you cross that fence?"

Teacher Sheshappa attempted to induce some interest into the class with a remark of cricket in his political question. Of course, cricket has always been a favorite game of all the classes. All it requires is a stick and a spherical object. The rules of the game are kind of open source and they are modified as per the requirements of the players. Sheshappa seemed to had understood this fact very well. His skill to lure the class with the bait of the word cricket appeared to had worked. A susurrus murmur followed and longed for a while. Most of us expected Nilesh to stand up and educate the class about the war and peace in his croaky voice, nonetheless it didn't happen. Though, I had the idea of why the Kargil war was fought, and how the Pakistani troupes infiltrated into Indian positions, I didn't vent to answer it due to an unknown reason, might be because of my sulky mood. Before the teacher could articulate his next fragment of speech, perhaps about the significance of Line of Cross in the border, a greying man with a *lungi* draped above his knees, wearing a red stained white undershirt, masticating the *paan* stormed in rage into the class and began yelling in no time,

"How dare you repeat it, you bastard, is that what you learn here? Deliberately repeating the same mistakes? You filthy whore-son, I had warned you just last month. Come what may, this time I have decided not to release that brute until you compensate the loss with the penalty. Tell your mother and father that I have captured and detained it. You filthy scums, shameless sons of bitches. I will teach you a lesson this time." His glare could burn the entire class. With the blood red mouth he looked like a mythic monster. He adjusted his whip on his colossus shoulder before striding out like a wild beast. That stubby forefinger of his with the acuminate grey nail, pointed towards me for every word that he uttered, stabbed at my heart from the distance. The whole class was stunned, including the teacher. A sort of shockwave had passed through the room. He appeared and disappeared in a series of windows as he passed along the corridor. Teacher released his tongue and the suppressed-breath once the man vanished from the sight. Every pair of eyes in the class navigated their way towards me. That long strange silence was a new experience for everyone. The man had certainly ruffled the feathers of teacher as well.

"Laxman Chalavadi, please getup. From now on, you need not come to school, at least to my class. If you really want to do so, please do get a letter from your father to the chairman. And get the permission from headmaster in written. You may leave now..." he ordered with a controlled anger and annoyance. I got to my feet and walked out with a face colored by a deep mortification, and didn't dare to see the faces of anyone else in the class including Swathi's.

Sun proved to be an all-weather enemy to me. He burned all along without an ounce of sympathy. I crossed the fence from east gate and began trudging in the gloomy lands, in the furrows of turmoil. I was impaled by the horns of the dilemma at every step, on whether to go to Desai's or to father or mother or towards the unknown.

I steered my way instinctively towards the *Dharmashale,* which was located at the edge of the field and along the main road. I paused and took a respite near the water-pump in its backyard as it occurred to me that I was thirsty from years. I helped myself; had to stroke the searing handle three or four times for a handful of water. Though I succeeded in quenching my thirst by lifting up the water from the crust of earth, I had ended up developing the blisters in my palms. *Dharmashale* was once a public shelter, especially for the travelers, and then it was used as an Inn by a Nepali Gurkha, the only foreigner whom I got a chance to witness then. Soon after his quick departure — owing to the penurious nature of villagers — the men of the likes of my father used the place as an adda to play cards and for their drink parties and even to make illicit love in the night. Eventually, its roof verging towards the right, shedded all of its tiles on a stormy night as it couldn't bear the heaviness of sins. In the aftermath, a new guest dwelled in there in that wretched house and had given birth to four adorable babies. I with the help of Ishwar had brought one of the new-borns to my home with an idea of adoption. That seemed to be the most winsome puppy among all for it resembled a panther cub. I hid him in the corner in a bamboo basket and fed with the milk that night in secrecy. By the sunrise, he was disappeared mysteriously. Mother had left him far away beyond the dump yard, and had ended the matter with a sarcastically metaphoric dialogue — "A hungry stomach should crave for the food but not for the flowers to decorate the hair." No one lived there now, save for the pigeon droppings, a heap of roof tiles and a rusty wind chime that tinkled now and then to remind one about his bearings.

As I treaded further in the endless fields in a deep quandary, water tank in the distance, looked like a lighthouse for a lost sailor, hinting where to proceed further. A boy whose name I had learned recently, arrived towards me after his words, "What's up Lachya, I heard Desai has captured your buffalo; he is a rogue and an inglorious son of a bitch. People should teach him a lesson. I have a secret about him, but I haven't revealed it to anybody yet. Your father went to take care of Kaali, you need not worry," he spoke it all in one go. I stood gazing at him weighing his words, and sniffing the authenticity in them.

"Really? Has my father gone to talk to Desai?"

"Yes, I just saw him going up there crossing the hedgerow. Your buffalo is at the upper plot, near his shed. I suspect that he might have beaten her badly with the whip or even chipped her rump with his sharp axe,"

I couldn't enunciate any words in return. The picture of Desai brandishing his axe flashed before my inner eye again.

"Have you seen my goats?" he asked, swinging a rope knot in his hand.

"No I haven't," said I, petrified by my own visions of Kaali's fate.

"They are not mine in fact; they belong to Inamdar's. That old midwife leaves them with my herd. They aren't used to the herding yet; confused creatures. They must have made their way towards home. That's why; I don't agree to join up such unsocials to my herd. What to do? We are too vulnerable for someone to take us for granted; we are too young to protest. She beguiles my mother and convinces her somehow, such a vexatious creature she is…"

He spun the knot of rope again dexterously and made his way through the yielding furrows ploughed recently. His tanned complexion, desiccated lips, sweaty forehead, dusty curly hair, an amulet of lord Hanuman resting in the neck, were all seemed to be complimentary for a guy of his milieu. Gopal — a signature boy of the region, synonymous to the northern plateau of vast expanses of dark barren flat lands, had worked as a free informer for me that day.

I couldn't find my bearings immediately after his departure, and found myself again on the crossroads of the day, equidistant to all different destinies that could end my day with wide variant results — home, school, Desai's farm and mother's workplace.

Where to go? Figure of Gopal receded behind the school in the distance into an unknown. One has to make a decision before the choices erode — I considered and made my way back towards the classroom from behind the building, to wait by the window outside, to seek through the bars, lurking like a thief.

"How many of you want to join the army? Well, in childhood everybody wants to become a soldier but while one grows up, his preferences change according to his world view. After a certain age, it's possible that one thinks patriotism is nothing but foolishness in the ages of globalization."

His muffled words became clear by and by as I sidled along the classroom. It's when I loitered and struggled to peep in partially into the window to have a sight of blackboard, he roared — "Do you think it's a joke? Don't you have any shame? Get lost."

He contorted his face into a scowl and shouted up till the roof teetered. On top, he ordered Ishwar to close the casement. My own friend, for whom I had run my breath out as a substitute runner while he batted like a king, shunned the window on my face. I was banished and was left with no option but to retreat. The circumstance compelled me to identify myself among the waste strewn along the windows — chewed-up pen caps, crumpled papers, mulberry seeds, pencil fans, candy wrappers, broken paper boats and all the things of that sort.

A journey of an outcast to a casted-off had begun.

I trudged back through the same hot soil, with an epithet of *persona non grata* inscribed on my forehead. Like a stray dandelion with no purpose, floating in the air only to land somewhere, I ambled in the fields for the rest of the day. Whiled my time away with few younger children who were engaged in collecting neem seeds with the vigor of a competition. Rani and I had already tried a hand at it. You get one rupee and a half for five kilograms of them. Mehboob was the man who used to stockpile the seeds in his backyard, loads and loads, large heaps of them lay rotting until he exported them in lorry loads. An extraordinarily rancid smell that emanated from those mounds blocked the senses of everyone around. All the passersby covered their nose and cursed Mehboob for his contribution to their nausea.

"Good that this bastard's house is at outskirts; else he would have scented the entire village with his mounds of hell."

Several of them even went on to vomit in many instances. I wondered what on earth he did with those giant loads of decaying seeds. 'They prepare soaps and oils with them. He exports the seeds to the factory for a higher price' — Rani had answers ready for everything under the sun.

School bell had rung a while ago. Birds began retreating to their nests. The hot earth was turned cold in no time. Sun was suspended into the knife like orange strips. I helped those boys to lift their accumulation to their shoulders and heads; too young shoulders for those weights.

At long last, I reached home late in the evening, to attend to my duties; however, I was welcomed by a haunting emptiness. No one was to be found at home, even Dyami. I fumbled around the shack, through the barn and inside the gate of veterinary clinic.

My pulses rose and dropped, and the legs trembled in bewilderment, like they did always. I got inside the home and turned on the lights. *'Where on earth could all be gone? It was Kaali alone who got detained. How about Dyami? Had she lost? And what about mother?'* amidst the proliferation of hounding questions, my hunger was awake out of the blue to persuade me to eat some *nucchu* i.e jowar porridge froze in the bottom of a clay pot. It was cold and sour, though was placed on earth oven. Cinders must have calmed down in the silence of home. I sought for some sort of a side dish to dilute its sourness. Mother used to cook the porridge with buttermilk instead of plain water, to make it an independent recipe and also with the idea to preserve it for the next day, lest father leaves off his share. It turned out unbearably sour that evening, as sour as my frame of mind, like the stale curd.

The sour gloom shifted to bitter after I realized that the photograph of Ramanujan which was stuck on wall was torn out apart, and only the quarter of his face remained — the whole of the man was turned into fractions. I unrolled the straw mat and lay on it, gazing blankly at the torn portrait of the mathematician. Between the two sunsets, my life was throttled by the grave uncertainties. The cold breeze brought in loads of pains, qualms and shivers at once. I seemed drowsy and was drifted into the sleep before long.

Clouds must have moved in the sky; stars must have formed and died; leaves must have fallen from the sacred fig; dogs must have barked out till the god consoled their throats into the silence of the void; the infant at the end of the street must have had its last cry of the night; And the mirabilis must have given birth to new buds reticently. Swathi must have waited long for a glance of me before going to bed.

"You filthy scum, why don't you sell me instead? Who is that scoundrel dared to buy her ? For what price did you sell? Sell me, go auction me tomorrow, I will become a whore. Where those animals are now, tell me. You son of a bitch tell me," I heard my mother yelling at father — holding his shirt collar and lifting him up from the charpoy for sure, interrogating in her style. Her invective followed a deep sound of a bottle breaking on to a rock. I presumed that she must have snatched and smashed his *old-monk* bottle to the step-stone. She bellowed and cried; a squall of a baby at the end of the street and a dog bark chorused her. She must have wiped off her snot with the edge of her saree and sneezed multiple times before saying,

"That little bastard behaves as though he is going to change the world with his studies. Both of you, go put me in the grave alive…I know some day you will surely do." In the fullness and emptiness of time, I heard her whimpers and snivels fading out steadily. I sensed her entering the door, and expected a fracas to break out with me, for the irresponsibilities and wrong deeds from my end. But to my surprise, she did not even vent to wake me up. As for me, I pretended to be asleep from a long time. After gulping a throat-full of water from the pitcher, she lay on her straw-mat like a wounded beast and had her leftover sobs before drifting into the slumber. I pulled my blanket over and concealed inside my tattered cocoon.

Three souls, though the knots in the same string, thought in different directions and slept in varied orientations like the angles of a triangle.

It's merely a matter of time for the time to contrive the stillness, and that's what it did then. In a matter of few snores, it was all ghost quiet. It must be midnight then, there were no snorts but only the croaks of frogs and the barks of dog, now and then like the dark coughs of a senile sick man. The breeze obstructed by the thin bamboo walls made eerie whistling sounds between the spells of silence. Somewhere deep down in my mind, an idea sprouted. The idea of brave men. The idea that worked for all the sages and the sinners, the kings and the paupers, the idea of flying, the idea of setting oneself free. One is bound to get possessed by such an idea when all the doors are closed or a charming door, bigger than all of them is wide open — I had made my mind to leave the home before the sunrise.

Chapter 9

After a little hum and haw, I slump into the oblivion of sleep, like a heavy pebble drowning deeper and deeper into a night sea with no clue of the depth. That doze should be a real one. I wake up by two knocks at the door, as they thud on the grounds of my drowsiness like colossus cannon balls. My eyes open warily and the gaze shifts in the direction of the door. It's too dim to see anything, too hazy to make out. The pattern of the knock matters, was it her? I hesitate to change my composure; reluctance and anxiety, seize my legs together. My eyes shut close bypassing my consent.

I contemplate under the fallen sky of the blanket. There emerges a circumstantial obligation to recall her. The very thought of the woman, paints a tantalizing picture on the canvas of my mind — undressed, lying on the bed, eyes wide open that chase the unknown shores. The enticer in me whines on my palms for not caressing her tender bottoms enough, for not fondling her satiny arms enough. The jasminy odor of her that pervaded my being, during every single nuzzle of mine to her silken neck, still there, persists in the pillow beside me. I place my face onto it and drown again in her aroma, swooning. The manliness arises in no time to remind me of its existence and the role. That flame of passion flickers and firms on its own. The desire is all set to lead me to her door. The ambition to own her for the night for one last time, is ready to ring the bell of her door. *Come what may, I want to win and lose with her for one last instance.* I yearn to devour off the bottle of nectar till the last drop for one last encounter. *It's time to pay out the residues and make good the regrets*, says within me, the burning alacrity. My fantasy takes a shape before long. I give a serious thought to approach her now.

I hear the knocks again, not with the rhythm of 'shave and haircut two bits' but odd, three plain taps. *Though unfamiliar, it must be her*, says my heart. People change, so their ways and beats. I grope my way towards the door in that murkiness, disturbed by the intermittent streaks of light that invade through the curtain breaches from far off nocturnal vehicles.

I unlatch the door, the door to the heaven, with all the accumulated fervor. But then, I meet with a bizarre sight, due to which, my heart ceases to pound all of a sudden and the darkness grips till I suffocate. A severe strike of cataplexy collapses me instantly like the shatter of a house of cards. I struggle to regain my vision. It's not her but him, with those two dark disks covering his eyes, in that darkest of the night. He sets foot into my room with the gait of a gangster and then she follows in his lee. He gets himself seated on the chair and grins at my trembling calves. She hovers next to me competing with my tremor. "I heard you are an expert. Let's see your skills, go make love to her, let me see," he orders it nonchalantly. As though, he is asking me to take a photograph of her. She undresses herself deftly and waits for me. I coerce myself to forget him and the gravity of the situation for a moment and proceed to move my bulk on to hers. I pierce her surface and stir her interior, as though the earth shakes; she flutters and rubs my ears and cheeks till they get blood red. I quake the earth again, she moans and whimpers, and then pants and gazes at the fan endlessly. As I endure, pursue and perpetuate further, the whole room levitates in the air. After a while, as though a large tree falls on to the ground, following a hurricane, we fall apart. There is a collective deep sigh, post the climax. I pant and gaze at her triumphant, she stares at him, and I follow her stare. It's him on the chair flourishing a pistol in his hand. He sneers and shoots her in the point blank. There's a buzzing in my ears for some time. Beyond that buzzing, all seems wildly still. I wipe her blood off my eyes to figure out his image on chair. He still holds that deceptive smile on his face; his profile gets red now and then, when the streaks of light cast on his face. He lifts up his pistol and his finger embraces the trigger, I want to speak, I want to say —

"I need to tell my story to the world before I die, please spare me. Once I am done, I will wait for you here, to die, by the second bullet in your Pistol." Like the Cow in the story of *Punyakoti*, that pleads the tiger to spare her, I want to plead him to spare me, nonetheless I don't. He shoots at me and the pain splits my skull into pieces. I fall dead beside her the very next moment. I become one with the stillness around.

The life flows through the nerves like never before. I come to know somehow, that I don't die. I rise up and turn on the lights. There is no blood, there is no pain, there is no one else in the room save for my shadow. I rinse my wet shorts and hang them to dry. An unknown motive drives my way towards the window. My hands dare to slide the curtain, but it gives in. Still, the blue light penetrates through the fissures and gives my face a midnight bath.

I toss myself up and down, refuge under the blanket and lose miserably. *Is man a paradox of misery? Is he the king of chaos? Is he the prime example of self-annihilation?* I ogle at the fan and then at the door. It's all stock still. I console and convince myself that there weren't any real knocks but these are all the tricks of the deceptive mind. *He cries and consoles himself, he dreads and soothes himself, man is certainly a paradox.* I forebode, agitate and pretend my sleep. It starts drizzling; now I hear the soft knocks at my window as well. As the rain intensifies, its pattering rhythm alleviates me into a trance. I wide open the screen and recline awake on the bed staring at the window frame. Many fleecy clouds wipe the face of the moon and sidle away. He glistens and the clouds move on.

There's a dawn in everyone's life, on which, one wakes up a man. I stepped out in the twilight with my resilient and all-purpose satchel on the back. The only witness of my expedition was the Lucifer. The crescent moon was busy roving through the blues of the sky. The black and white world was engaged at the climax of colorful dreams. Like a wayfarer, I took the road towards railway station. The mist and the silence exhilarated my senses. The huge banyan tree looked like a silhouette of a mother breastfeeding her baby. As I treaded few yards, my temples became effervescent; I was woken up by a dream — of Ishwar, shunning the windows on my face. It was cruel indeed. *All you could close is a window but not the door of my life.* I pondered like a brave man. I am not sure from where such audacity was stemmed in me. *Men get brave by the brave actions, they win over their fear by understanding the nature of fear*, and I defended my decision by formulating my own philosophy.

I did not have a faintest inkling of where was I heading to. The only answer that I concocted in my mind for the moment was to walk. A walk for the freedom, a walk to the unknown. I was indeed brutal in chopping down rest of the thoughts that sprouted in disguise of answers.

Few dogs at the end of the street stared at me warily pricking their ears and widening their drowsy eyes. I sustained my firm march through them like an insider. After a thorough scrutiny of my person, they pricked and dropped their ears mutely to resume their naps, to join back the dreams of dog world. I must have looked familiar and congenial to them in their eyes, perhaps like an alien empathizer.

In every life, there are certain decisions that seem strange at the later point of time. You realize that you didn't make those decisions but you are made for those decisions. Teacher Chaitanya always quoted — 'You do not choose this existence but the existence chooses you'. Such resolutions that create 'What if's' in the later part of life are the coordinates that educe a sense of 'predestined' for life. That sunrise proved to be such decisive coordinate of my life.

As I drew near railway station, a deep whistle of train violated the decorum of the silence of the daybreak, hitting hard at my thought process. The train seemed to had arrived in the station and I began running halfhearted to catch it, and manifestly it was a miss. Did I miss it deliberately? Again I am not sure. It is more likely that we miss, when anything is done halfhearted. Perhaps I had found a purpose for my walk, to walk faster and to transform the walk into a run, with an alibi to catch the train.

Few passengers who got down happened to be of my village. Those faces that are not fully registered in your memory, but you know that you have come across them somewhere, sometime, like the extras in cinema — the bystanders in your journey. I chose to be furtive by hiding myself in the shadow of a massive pillar at the entrance of the station. I liked British for that matter; all that they built are as strong and monumental as their barbarism. The next train seemed to be only after four hours or so. Did it really matter? Was I considering the option of departing in train? To where? Without a ticket? Mind grew fecund for the questions and chaos. I paused there in the clutches of indecision and waited for my heaving chest to calm down. The train chugged further and roared louder as it disappeared in a distance.

It occurred to me that there's no point in waiting there for a train to which I will not be boarding. I stepped out through the garden gate and made my way past the station through the treeless, hopeless wide open moor that lead to a hitherto blue hill.

Laal's *Tonga* that carried the surprise bearing passengers, rattled down the road, scooted and vanished at the bend. The horse was too old and emaciated for the fate it had to carry. It should be the reincarnation of Nietzsche's Turin Horse in all senses. My loath towards the coachman Laal was subdued by the pity on his horse. It groaned, grumbled and wept but all within itself, under its eye-plates. I empathized with the horse and nurtured a thought for its providence, *why can't it run away and free itself from the clutches of that ruthless and grumpy Laal?* But I dropped the idea as the next question popped up — *run away to where?* The cart had already faded away, so did the image of old horse, its swollen knees, tattered crest and the worn-out shoulder.

Transformation of the black and white world into the hues of color was inconspicuous a phenomena. Golden sun had begun his glorious show. Even after covering a fair distance, I did not consider or ask myself, to where and till what extent that I am going to march just like that. Had I taken right from the railway station, I would have reached national express-way by now, but I hadn't. Even in that case, if I had reached express-way, would I be boarding a lorry of a stranger destined to Mumbai? I neither believed nor doubted my conviction. All I was concerned for the moment was to walk. Every time, the holes in my chappals let in any pointy stone or a thorn, I had to stop to see about it and it was only those encounters that could pause me.

When it comes to the question of experience, in another instance from the past, I had hiked with my mother and Kaali across all the surrounding villages and farms, possibly ten miles or so, in the quest of a male buffalo to get Kaali conceived. Other than that, I don't recall any other example where I had to trek for longer distances. So, did it mean I can't create a new example now? All the great things are not done, but happen — I found my retrospection in regards to the experience bemusing, injudicious and at times ludicrous. The fact of my inexperience did not perturb me much, but the misgivings about where was I heading to and what I will be doing there, these very uncertainties tormented me like the unreachable sores in the back.

In a little while, I found myself pacing towards the hill that never failed to enchant me during my terrace vigils, and compelled me to sketch it every time that I happened to witness it above the skyline. It was the same hill that I recalled in my geography classes, in every occasion that the teacher referred to a mountain or a hilly terrain. In other words, it was the first hill figurine that was etched in my permanent memories. *Well, are there any permanent memories as such?*

In the distance, up the hill there perched a white edifice with a green flag waving over. An unknown impulse lured my feet to progress towards it. There were steps laid for pedestrians straight to the top of the hill and were painted in white with lime-wash. It looked like a minute pallid line from 'my terrace' back home. The serpentine muddy road around the hill tended to prove that the summit had access by motor vehicles as well. It wasn't blue as it looked from my place. There were small bushes on either sides of the way and the hill was dotted with scrubs except for few dwarf trees. Towards my right in the distance were few herds of sheep that looked like the speckles of curd on brown plains. Then again, to convince myself, my mind had found a target to walk, to reach the summit, a purpose for walk but after that? What to be done after reaching the brow of the hill? I didn't bother to ask the question nor had I any clue of the answer.

It is engraved in the very genes of the human being, to climb the mountain despite knowing that there's nothing to be done after making it to the summit. Mountains and hills exist to be climbed. Man is used to it from the ages. So did me. That's how my conscience defends my childhood adventure.

After making it half the way, I seated myself on the steps for a breather, under the shade of an unknown dwarf country tree that leaned over the path. I noticed several seeds and dry peels of *seethaphala*, strewn beside the steps. Anybody could postulate that the hill must be a home for custard apples. The brown swaying grass on both the sides shimmered in the sun as the gusts of the wind generated the waves. There was tall grass here and there, brown and dying green around small and big boulders that looked like toppings to the hill. An immediate sentence emerged and receded in the mind — *mother would have prepared not less than ten broomsticks with one patch of such grasses.*

As I surveyed back towards the path that I treaded, spire of railway station looked picturesque. Beyond that, far in the distance, twenty or thirty whips away from the station, my village appeared like a hidden hamlet obscured in the crater, waiting to be discovered. The water tank and the *godown* stood tall and distinct. There, near that water tank, in an isolated shack, my mother must be getting ready, wrapping her scythe up in her old *saree* and two roties for the lunch. My father must be praying to goddess Dyamavva with an incense stick in hand creating circular wisps before the portrait of goddess, seeking better luck for rest of the day. Both of them were deep asleep during my flee. Even if they were awake, would they care to stop me? Though I bought the notion of 'not sure', my conclusion inclined towards a clear No. At the adda, Chennappa must be halting the vehicles and passersby demanding his toll. It must be the prayer time at school. Nilesh must be reading out today's headlines from the newspaper with a handkerchief in his left hand. Swathi must be standing at last in the line, blinking her sparkling eyes and smiling for no reason. She must have searched for me in the adjacent line and should be hoping for my arrival, at least post the prayer, the way I did most of the times.

And Kaali?

Chapter 10

I had indulged myself into studying math on that bright and tranquil noon, sitting in veranda leaning my back against the wall, attempting to spread my roots into the bowels of the hill on the sunny day. A fork tailed drongo that perched on a young branch of the sacred fig, in the right corner of the front-yard was trying to say something through a variety of strink-strink sounds. Did it try to speak to me? To a new guest to the place who supposedly does not seem like a guest? Or was it a signal for someone? There were many of them near my house as well, but had never cared to notice them so intensively before — a boon of being in solitude, a privilege to experience the perspiration and impulse of the mother nature. Those cherry-red eyes, glossy black body and the tale that looked like the tale of a kite, constituted to what could be called a paragon of the creator's novelty.

I turned over the leaves in my math book with dexterous movements of the fingers for no subtle reason, like the nature's act, like the dance of a creeper, like the course of a river, does it need a reason? In the midst of the solemn silence, pastoral folk song of a shepherd boy sounded rapturous. There flowed a stream of honey in that vast aridness, trinkling down on to the deepest corners of my soul, drop by drop, gliding the sweetness. There was a rhythm between the silence and the song, like that of the breast and the baby, evading the realm of time. I had no idea of the lyrics that he sung, it didn't make any sense to my then puerile intellect, but that was all needed for that moment to lift me up into the heavens.

It was only the intense consistent cough of Ajja, that choked me up from that engrossing affair. I swiftly filled up a glass of water from an old copper pitcher, which had diamond shaped patches of polish, and held it before him. He rose up to sit on bed and partook with all the grace though in his disheveled state, and threw an indiscreet smile, acknowledging his temporary contentment. His long, ethereal, furry, silvery beard deserved an elegant comb. While he clutched the glass between his obscure lips, his moustache used to get a cold bath every time as it filtered the water adding its own essence before it reached his throat. Though his mouth hidden under the facial hair, one could never fail to notice his ever-flowering smile. One also could easily be puzzled to make out, whether his eyes looked radiant due to the glowing facial hair or it was a case vice versa. Before receiving the glass back, a lady's voice calling, "Daada," emerged from the main door, merely a door frame without the hinges or doors, at the end of the front yard. Ajja commended me with his nod and an idiosyncratic gesture swaying his left hand. I hurried to the entrance with a prance like Dyami.

A woman wearing a veil over her head, waited to hand a large plateful of dishes over to me, covered in a thin green cloth, assuring — "It contains a share for you too!" with a twinkling beam. I threw back a sheepish smile in place of a 'thank you' and brought the laden plate inside with the adroitness of a butler to place it on an ancient table in Ajja's room, sensing the formation of a question in mind — should we wait till it's time? Or till the hunger itself rings at us?

The summit had a Dargah with a walled front-yard of the size of a mini playground. Though the high walls and the door frame installed at the front made it look like an incomplete structure, the vegetation nurtured over the years in the garden filled the atmosphere with the colors and freshness of life.

In the shrine was a grave of a nameless Sufi mystic, who happened to be the pupil *peerazad* of Gaisu Daraaz, a well known Sufi saint of Chishti order. Next to the shrine was a small stark room for the curator Ajja. A fascinating bust of a white horse present in the shrine was the silent cynosure of the place. I had made space for myself in the veranda beside the doorway to Ajja's room. Almost like a self-appointed sentry to the fortress of Dargah, who extended his role also to a loyal manservant to Ajja unsolicitedly.

When I found myself at the loose end, that afternoon, Ekalavya had knocked the door of my mind. He reminded me of the efficacy of self-study and discipline. The way he made a clay statue of Drona and esteemed it as his guru, I framed a statue of Ekalavya in my mind and began venerating him as an idol — the master of hope. I made my mind to study the stuff by myself and began to solve math problems and learnt few theorems. *When the earnest Ekalavya was rejected by Drona for his non silver-spoon backgrounds, he must have walked away into the isolation like me* — I defended my act of flee and blatantly shifted its responsibility on to the shoulders of my then imaginary guru Ekalavya — *it was him who seeded a thought in me inconspicuously of leaving home without giving it a due consideration.* His culpability was weighed by my reliquence. I rose up to replenish another glass of sweet water as his cough seemed to augment with time.

It appears to be the next day or perhaps the next to that, when the same lady with the veil over her head visited us; she waited at her regular place under the shade of a greyish green tamarind tree located outside at the entrance to the front-yard. As I went to receive her generous food offerings, I wanted to ask, "Why do you stand here outside? Why can't you come inside?" In the contrary, she began enquiring me with her own curious eyes and the concerned brows,

"How is he now?"

I replied blankly, "He is good."

She shifted her gaze from me to the frame of the door through which she could catch a glimpse at the pointy leaves of sacred fig shimmering under the sun and swaying for the music of wind, and vented to say, softening her voice —

"Just let us know if anything happens,"

I looked at her, deadpan.

"He might die anytime, he is living with cancer. Just let us know if anything happens…"

"Okay,"

"If you feel it hard to climb down, just wave that flag, or just hoist it over there atleast."

She indicated towards the top right corner of Dargah and left the place. I gazed at her with the heavy plate and heavier heart in hands till she receded into the slope of the hill-brow breaking the mirage all through her way.

I stood petrified for a moment, but as soon as I turned back to make my way into the door of front-yard, my auditory senses grew alert to a song of a shepherd which seemed going on for a while, the words were a little clear this time — *neelangi thottakondu, jattikudala bittakondu, ninthaano mallayya…*

The rough translation of the song goes like,

'He who wears the blues, he who streams the tresses of *jata*, stands in your way, what do you say, what do you ask...'

I have come to believe recently that It must be about Shiva — a Hindu deity. I was too young to decode and understand the songs then, rather too naive and novice to the sphere of art. *When the god himself, stands in my way, what will I say? Or what will I ask for? For the immortality? Or of my own future? Or for the supreme knowledge? Or the question of, where will I go if I die? And why did you send me to the planet earth without assigning a clear goal, without mentioning the proper terms and conditions?* I have no idea even now, of what to ask for, since the life doesn't seem like anything to be asked for. Though it sounds part serendipitous, part enigmatic, part in control, part intractable, it seems like a game to be played void of the knowledge of rules.

As I placed the plate deftly, my gaze navigated towards the corner of Ajja, where he dwelled most of the time. On an old ivory-cream straw-mat, in the midst of even older books and papers strewn all around, he looked like a fragile creature crumpled in the blanket. *What else should he look like? After-all a man counting his days, after-all a man who would soon be slumbering in the grave undisturbed, after-all a man who would be rotating with the earth, abiding by the laws of nature, without displaying any sort of resistance, being one with the air and one with the fire, one with the silt and one with the sky. I am bestowed upon with the most significant task — to inform them if anything happens.* I began to rewind and brood over the conversation that I had with the lady. *What is it meant to die? His breath would stop, he wouldn't speak, and he would just lie dead. I have to be mature enough to close those deep and radiant eyes, if they remain unshut even after the bird in his chest flew away. He will be an empty cage; there won't be any fluttering afterwards.*

I had no noticeable intimacy with death then except that of an old lady near my house. One Sunday morning, when the bat bearer Ishwar didn't arrive at the playground, I was assigned with the task by the team to bring him or at-least his bat. As I went to his door, there lingered an unusual and forced silence. Faint murmurs emanated from inside the house. I was always timid and jittery to call out anyone loudly, as nobody liked us to play cricket all the day under that raging sun. I hovered around the door for a while and peeped in through the window like a neighbor's cat. Ishwar happened to catch a glimpse of me immediately. Cats smell the cats. He looked wary and gestured towards me to wait, with his pursed lips. I cornered myself outside and waited patiently for his arrival. There was no sign of his appearance even after minutes, but few people began to swarm in, one by one, manifestly uninvited. I moulded some courage and made my way into the house behind few elderly villagers. Before long, I realized that his granny was on her death bed. *When does one decide that she will breath her last in a while? How do they decide that it's her death bed?*

From the fringes of the assemblage, embracing a sticky wooden pillar, I sought the view of his granny. A weak shaft of light had fallen on her face from the barred skylight window. Still, her gaze was stiff towards the ceiling and the toothless mouth was wide open. Several houseflies were alighting now and then on and around her chin, and were chased by the hands of Ishwar's mother. The breath from that mouth made a strange noise, "hrr brr..hrr..brr…". One of the elderly man from priest community, asked Ishwar's mother to bring the holy water — *Gangaajala*. She hurried up and brought down a tiny bronze-made antique cup in no time. The man poured the water into the granny's hollow mouth gracefully. The water obstructed the rhythm of 'hrrr…brrr…' and all the eyes around were witnessing the spectacle with an extraordinary curiosity. All waited for the old lady to cease her breathing. All waited for the flitting bird in her threadbare chest to fly away into the boundless cosmos. It was a moment of realization for me that like a birth, death also happens to be a mystifying phenomenon. The dier along with the seers waited together for the arrival of the god of death. Her wheeze intensified suddenly and the people around lifted themselves up onto their toes. I felt someone pinching my elbow from behind. It was Ishwar as I inferred. He beckoned me out with a mumble. He already had managed to smuggle the bat outside and had rested it on the pyol. In the haste, we began to march towards the playground, leaving behind a kind of turbulence.

"Bicycle punctured," he said concerned.

"All are waiting," I replied.

We walked briskly towards the main road. With the bat leaping along his legs, it seemed like he walked with three limbs. Ishwar was too proud for his bat which bore a sticker of *kookaburra*. He always boasted with a remark, 'Ricky Ponting uses the same bat'. Rather, it was certainly a fact that his bat had earned him some hangers-on at the ground.

As we moved past the water tank, an old lady with a metal pail on her waist, emerged on to the road from the *dobhighat*, a local laundry bay.

"Boy, what are you up to? Where are you heading to?"

"To the ground, to play," replied Ishwar quickly. The lady seemed to had ignored my existence.

"You can play cricket every day, but you can see your granny only today for the last time, why don't you be home?" she said crossing us, throwing a scowl. Ishwar looked unperturbed and strode further.

"My mother said, that she observed granny murmuring about the visions of Yamraj riding a buffalo-bull manifesting on the wall beside her bed…"

I did not know what to say in return or ask. I formed some appreciative inquisitiveness on my visage and pretended my finest, to not to disappoint his story. The moment he said, buffalo-bull, it reminded me of the giant bull that I had witnessed during Kaali's conception ceremony. *If it had to carry the old and fat Yamraj on its back, it must be even heftier than the one I had seen*, I thought.

"My mother cooked granny's favorite dish *upma* this early morning and fed her. Dying people eat a lot as they have to set off on a long journey," he repeated what his mother must have told him.

"Your granny was dying?" I asked in an innocuous tone.

"Yes, today she will. I heard mother and father discussing this daybreak. She never moved an inch from her bed from past fifteen days. Mother took care of her food and ablutions every day. I too helped sometimes to lift her up and make her sit and recline."

I maintained the conversation till we reached the playground, merely to keep him engaged. Such an incomparable fellow, for the sake of our match, he was ready to get beaten up by an old umbrella from his father for his absence at his post on an extremely important day back home.

Later that evening, we witnessed from the playground the wafts of smoke rising up into skies and heard the sounds of the crackers bursting and the brass bands playing about the locus of Ishwar's home. And only then Ishwar was summoned to home, to attend to his obligations as a member of the family. I was entrusted to keep his bat for the night.

Ajja never behaved like a dying man. Apart from his afternoon naps, he lived sprightly with the spirit of a young deer all through the day — agile and inquisitive. He remained vibrant by indulging himself in some or the other stuff like nurturing the plants, reading, scribbling; he even went for quick errands about the hill for leisurely strolls and also to fetch the herbs.

I climbed up the stairs of Dargah to see the place where the red flag to be hoisted if 'something happens'. And from there, the house of that lady looked diminutive. *She said let us know, that implies, she must have other members as well at home. Is she the daughter of Ajja? Or his daughter in law?* I kept speculating with my unproven mind. The dry wind of the afternoon that stirred me had brought in a bit of homesickness at the edge of my awareness. It's something that can't be defined; it's not actually the homesickness but a thought that arises out of aversion towards the situation or the place at certain time, a kind of sensitive intermittent distaste. I never brought it into the frontline of the mind to fight and win over. In the later part of life, I learned that there are few thoughts in everyone's mind, that are supposed to be preserved like a family heirloom, though they are obsolete, though they aren't of much use or the significance, just to be placed in a dark corner not to erase their existence. Like an abandoned rusty scooter in your street, which the owner doesn't want to sell and nobody wants to buy.

Every-time I visited Ajja's sanctum, a consuming fragrance of a wild jasmine made me linger for long. He must have stocked them before, they must have withered, dried up and evaporated by the enigma of time, but their fragrance remained there with the original intensity, like the recorded song of a dead singer. He owned a vintage radio but never cared to play it. 'There's no need of it anymore,' he had remarked — did he mean that he was too old to be amused by a radio? There was a locked door in his room that he never offered me to open and reveal. Its door was chipped at the base and I tried to have a glance by drooping down in his absence. The fragrance was even more intense at the door; it dominated the musty smell of old books dormant inside. All I could glance at with that contortion was : the legs of wooden racks, few orphan quills on ground bathed in dust, few rebel pages of texts unglued from their herd, and some traces of invasion by the gang of rats. It was also evident that the room had a tiny window at the other end — there was enough light spilled over.

At times, I rummaged for the key at his study area with a readymade answer, 'I thought to clean that room as it seems clumsy.' Nonetheless, it always kept the flame of my curiosity alive, the sealed room of an opaque man.

Chapter 11

There is only one season on top of the hill and it's of the solemn silence. Be it the golden beams of sun or the showers from the heaven, the summit harbors the privilege to experience it before anyone else. All that one could do from the pinnacle is to negotiate with those gargantuan cotton balls broke out from the belly of god's cushion, for a mizzle. However, when they glide away paying no heed, the endless sea of the blue emptiness looms over and obliges one to go inward infinitely. A lonely bird, dark and small, soars higher and higher, in the vast blue abyss, till it thinks that it has flown too far and there's nowhere else to go. It steadies its wings and decides to descend. At the halfway, a thought flashes again in its humble mind — 'what's there to be done at the ground? That too with these wings?' It makes an about-turn and soars again higher and higher. It repeats.

On that bright sunny morning, Ajja was digging up a hole next to a dusty *sapota* tree beside the floral hedge which was smothered along the walkway in the front-yard; I went and stood across him drooping, perhaps to lend a hand or to enjoy watching his excavation. "Fetch some water from the hand-pump," he spoke to my shadow that fell on the dig, quivering his fragile head like a string puppet. I did not ponder on anything as my mind seemed to be in a harmony with its host. It was not less than a challenge for me to differentiate between the saplings of guava, sapota and the mango. Whenever Ajja sent me to pick a specific sapling up from the little nursery that he nurtured under the sacred fig, I used to stand perplexed looking at them, like a mother looking for her baby among the newborn babies rested in the cradles in a hospital nursery. *When the life is young and innocen,t it all looks the same* — I had thought.

He had planted a mango sapling by the time I made my way back with a pitcher full of water over my shoulder. His beard ends were kissing the fresh and maiden shoots of the plant as he evened out the mud around it. The spectacle looked like the life coming in full circle, as both of its ends embraced each other. *A life about to end and a life about to begin. If there is anything that doesn't cease, it's called life. He was nurtured by the nature and he did nurture it back, a never ending tale of give-and-take* — I brooded. My mind took its own time to etch the scene as vividly as possible. Howbeit, my curiosity was different altogether. I decided to avoid hitting around the bushes and put forth my suspicion without an ounce of hesitance,

"You seem to study those matka charts much, but I have never seen you betting, why is that so Ajja?" I asked, avoiding the eye contact gazing at the semi wet mud, which was ready to womb a new life. There was a centipede crawling away from us in haste, as though it took us for extraterrestrials.

He prompted a reply with a smile fixing his gaze at the slithering worm, "For what grand purpose should I bet? What have I got here to do with wealth? I am like a feather floating in the air, neither driven by a purpose nor bound by an ambition. I am not sure of myself that, whether I will be alive for the supper or not. When I say 'I' it doesn't mean it's 'I' who is going. The one that goes is different from the one that stays forever. The goer never stays and the stayer never goes. We must understand the stayer with the help of goer and learn the goer with the assistance of the stayer."

He was done with the planting and leaving the son of departed centipede into my head with those abstruse words.

"Pour the water till they reach its soul, keep pouring."

He always spoke in a cryptic language which could only be understood by himself, and perhaps the drongo along with him.

"Then why do you study those charts so keenly and guesstimate the next numbers?" I asked brushing all of his greek and latin away. Like an authoritative interrogator.

"It's only to get some insights into the mind of the man who draws the numbers," —

I couldn't comprehend it again; I looked at him with a pale face. What did he mean by get some insights of the mind?

"Fetch some more water…" he said retiring to his chamber, rubbing off his wet hands to his moss green towel.

I whiled away my afternoon by stretching on the straw-mat arbitrating with a remote siesta. That fierce parching heat and the benumbing silence had stopped the rotation of the earth for a while. After a spell of stillness, it was awake again — the feeling of homesickness, like an obscure bushfire waiting for the wind. Before could it spread inconspicuously and grip me in its clutches, I dared to bring it into the vanguard to confront. I maneuvered and bulled further into myself only to realize that it's not merely the homesickness but a strange melancholy, a feeling of not being loved by anyone, a feeling of meaninglessness, a sense of emptiness. Inch by inch, I grew baffled by my deceitful sensitive nature. *That sacred fig, drongo, flowering hedges along the walkway and compound walls, Ajja, hitherto singing shepherd boy, his sheep, do they all feel the same? This entire hill, it should be here from unknown time, did it feel bad for itself?, leave about all, this entire earth, the so called pale blue dot in the cosmos, if at all it had a soul of its own, did it ever feel lost?* — I brooded.

Like an unforeseen arrow from an unknown direction, Ajja's untamed cough shook me all over. He coughed his chest out in a high pitch, and fell quiet instantaneously followed by a deep breath. I did not rise up but waited for another cough. I looked warily at the ceiling of veranda and pricked my ears. Seven, six, five, four, three, two, one. There was no sound. My legs trembled and I grew chary. The veiled lady had reminded me of his condition just hours ago. I began sweating and wanted to call up 'Ajja' loudly, even so, I hesitated to do that, thinking, it might turn into a grotesque embarrassment for me. I rose up slowly, like a cautious wild-cat, still waiting for a sound of a cough or a wheeze or a rumble of paper, to pinch the balloon of silence. I filled the water glass till it's brink with my ears still erect and carried it tiptoeing into his room. The incandescent bulb over his bed was held slackly by a worn out wire and kept hanging like a pendulum right over him, causing a rhythmic shadow light effect. It seemed to me that the bulb had no switch to turn it off, it spilled orange light all the time that it had the electric spirit running in its nerves. His chest heaved, his lustrous facial hair rippled by his deep taciturn breaths and his countenance looked thoughtful and content. The bird was still there in his rib-cage alive, fluttering, singing and nesting. His firm hands on the chest seemed guarding it at their best. There should be a gentle smile under that furry facial hair. His number charts, blunt pencils and large hard-bound title-less volumes napped beside him with the same grace. I loitered there for a while and did not bother to wake him up for the water, rather retreated to my place and gulped myself. As I stretched down again, the same thought of the blue abyss of futility resumed to trouble my mood, nonetheless my then imaginary Guru, Ekalavya had come to my rescue over again. I studied math and played with number charts towards the end — 'to get some insights into the mind of the man who draws the lottery'. My love for the numbers went on till the sheep in distance bleated their baa's and meh's in the gloaming. The shepherd also chorused them, for a lamb must have been trailing from the herd, which supposedly not weaned to the world yet.

Enough is enough. You take me for a retard? You judge that I am a coward? My furtive movements do not mean that I am afraid to confront you. You think I am terrified by him? Who is a snoop here, Me? You? Him? I can't behave like an infiltrator anymore around my own house. Don't you dare to be too smart. Why did you misinform me that you were divorced? Was it I who beguiled you? You think I am a Don Juan? It's you who knocked at my door, remember? It's you who narrated fairy tales to encroach into my bed. It's you who ushered an air of malaise into my life. I can't go through it anymore. Let's steer clear of each other, ok? Let's whip the things into a shape, let's settle this matter.

I read it myself, part in her shoes part as a third person. I feel it crude and puerile. I press the back space button and erase off the composed email.

Our flowers blossomed in the dusk and bloomed in the dark.

Our world swayed by the moon and cursed by the sun.

How long can we breathe the darkness, how long can we sing the berceuse?

I obliterate it again ruthlessly.

The straw in my hand stirs and pushes down the mint leaf subconsciously till the base, and the leaf blocks the mouth of straw and dares to obstruct my sip. The revenge is fair and natural, as natural as Newton's hair. I stir the mocktail and sip it again, as sour as ever before. My heart chases the unknown shore. I regret choosing a dim-lit, low ceiling, boxed cafe. *The depressed come here to get even more depressed* — I say within myself after a brief

                           Soman Gouda

survey of all the despondent eyes. The cowards in disguise, the fake rebels, the escapists, the mediocres — more of such words emerge and subside in me. *After-all you are one among them.* I pay the bill to a sweet girl for the sour drink and walk low-profile towards the exit, twiddling my cricket-hat, drifting through the forest of chaotic youth.

There's a world of difference with the world by the time I stepped out from the cafe. Pavements shimmered and the hands of guys were moved to their partners' waists and craved for even further. The world hankered for a warmth and a sense of longing seized the mysterious twilight. A haunting melancholia had unrolled its infinite mat all through the roadway and slumbered like nobody's business.

I make my way through the inebriated, stoned and rarely sober strollers warming my palms in pockets of my jacket like an expert perambulator. As I take the turn towards Imperial Street subway station, a gravitational pull exerted by a *paan* vendor benumbs me. I order a *paan*, and wait for his nimble hands to prepare it. He serves the readymade, fishing it out from his thermocol refrigerator. A betel-nut cone of a length of little finger is pierced by a tooth-pick like an arrow piercing the heart shape in the ideograph of a 'wounded heart'. The same tooth pick penetrated a complimentary cherry and skewered it with the *paan*. My mouth wells up before long as all of the salivary glands get ready for a new chemistry. Ingredients like gulkand, areca nut, lime, cloves, mukhwas blend together as I chew them in a rhythm to craft a whimsical mood. When most of the people in my village chewed *gutkha* and painted the roads, corners, electric-poles, tree trunks and walls generously with their spit, I wondered, why chew in first place if at all it is to be dribbled out of mouth. I realized later about the effects of these psychoactive traditions. (When I had to give my first presentation at my work, I had champed two chewing gums in washroom covertly to manufacture a sort of courage.)

I drift through the crowd and pull myself to sit on a step of an old book shop for no reason. *Paan* seems to have done its job. *The gross transformed into fine and the fine transformed into the subtle in the flash of time.*

I grow too casual, unpretentious and slovenly at once. Resting my chin on my palm, I contemplate at the strollers, and survey through an open cafe by the roadside in opposite lane.

Those apparitions, those streams of people, they all, yes, all of them are the victims of the so called eastern philosophy. They all are stemmed from one source? One universal law governs them all? They are all the same? It should be a conspiracy to nullify the brilliance of individual beauty — my mind swings and broods.

That French bearded chap who pose like a gentleman hiding his sins under the plastic smile, filtering all the crudeness at his protruding Adam's apple, has got something in his mind for the evening. That giggling plump lady must be lying to her new partner about her tastes, toning them according to his, by researching his virtual presence. That old man with young eyes, who steals the glances at curvatures of stroller women and nymphets, looks like a Humbert in search of a Lolita. That chi-chi tenderfoot there, muddling to take his girlfriend's breath away by speaking about Sherlock Holmes and his detective adventures, fails miserably and wipes the mud on his ungrown moustache. It's apparent that his naughty eyes fix at her young cleavage, he wants to ask her more but he doesn't. She seems to know all of his mischiefs and still tends to act as if unlearned and naive, spuriously appreciating the fictional English detective and showing proud for her boyfriend's sophisticated interests. That group at the right corner table breaks into an enormous guffaw, for every word they utter. A sort of laughing club of three girls and two boys, all of them still unclear on who is hitting on whom.

Then, my eyes begin a spell of scan towards a glassed café, towards the right in the same line. There, on the first table, through the glass wall, I see a man with shades busy slicing the garlic bread or something of that sort. I sink down into an unfathomable uneasiness. It's him! Opposite to him is a lady, (that may not be the right word) across from him is a lady helping him, showing her back towards me. That water-fall like hair, seem intimately familiar to my being. My heart goes its way off beam. I wait for a glance of her profile. My mouth dries up and I feel thirsty. I adjust my cap a little down after the confirmation and sidle into a dark alley.

So, she is normal, she is back in business with him. Let the peace prevail then. I take a deep sigh and disappear into the dark matter. So am I beating a hasty retreat now? What should I be afraid of? In fact this is what I had suggested her in one of our fornication sessions, to reconcile the conflict with him and to reunite eventually, but that's when she had delivered a long speech denying my commiseration and even had gone to an extent to deride me with the remark — 'You are a milksop'.

I stumble upon an old rusty bollard installed in the middle of that closed lane. Did it hurt? I brood on whom to blame for the mishap and grope further like a lost pet. A man smiles and invites me for a dance-bar through the backdoor. I evade him with a cursory no. Once a familiar alley is now turned into a strange zone. I rush and reach the end of the alley to join the main road that connects me to the subway station. I become one among the confused strollers again, but a little firm this time.

The sky train that passes over me like an arrow of silver light, reminds me of home. I board the train and break into the night sky. The windows turn into mirrors again. I reflect.

There seemed many parallel and mysterious streams flowing in me concomitantly, like the multicolored strands in a telephone wire buried in the belly of the earth. While I gazed at the strollers and vented on travesty and innuendos towards them, a subtle part of me, a piece of my heart must have searched for Swathi among those numerous faces. It seems to be the tendency of any heart to desire for a miracle in its own fantasized manner. Even beyond, in the back of my mind, I must have got tormented all through the evening about squandering my time and not progressing on my writing. Beyond all this, there seems to be a buried giant, indiscernible and absurd. It smells of melancholy, of nostalgia, of a forgotten dream, of a lost song, of a broken string in the violin, of a déjàvu. I may prove too wimpish and pigeon-hearted for the daunting task of digging it up now. However, my courage and conviction like an active volcano could erupt anytime exhuming all the corpses out, the living and the dead.

Chapter 12

The entire sanctum was engulfed in the soothing aroma of morning *Loban.* Curls of smoke were swimming in the air and rolling into somersaults like the astronauts floating in the space devoid of gravity. Shafts of sunlight were spread on the floor through the tiny window that had a complicated affair with sun. It closed itself and opened based on its mood and wish, like an involuntary organ of Darga. The liberated dry petals of chrysanthemums waited for the gusts of wind, to fly and get into life again, not as flowers but as butterflies. Peacock feathers were untied and scrambled on the floor behind the sculpture of the white-horse. They looked like the radiating blue eyes of god strewn all over. I was wallowed myself in assembling and binding them together. Wondered how could peacocks hold them all tightly together as a train in tail and perform those graceful yet oscillating dances to lure their partners.

The strips of light had grown long and were shining the shoulder of the horse. The massive statue was made of some fine wood — must be mahogany or mango. It must have been carved in pieces and then assembled. When I was too young, I always thought the same about man, that god carves limbs, stomach and head and then after assembling everything, he places the heart for some and he forgets for the rest. With its bridles and saddle, the stallion looked so alive as though it went out all the night around the hill with its master and secretly retreated to stand there at dawn as a statue to rest during the day. There was a ceremonial green shawl on its crest with golden embroidered border that twinkled and reflected whenever the sun negotiated for a ride with his brilliant shafts of light.

Murmurs of the leaves, musings of the flower hedges and the cacophonies of the native sparrows were all outshined by the song of the Drongo which had begun singing a cryptic verse before the shepherd boy could even prepare his throat for the day.

"Saheb, our daughter is severely ill. Suffering from ceaseless fever and my husband has lost his job recently. We cannot afford a doctor now. Could you please bless us with an amulet? We have no one else but you…" leaped in a strained voice of a lady from the veranda. I stooped down from the hind legs of horse to seek a glance at the visitors. The lady had rested her child on the right shoulder and her husband stood beside ducked, with a scruffy wired handbag sagging from his left hand.

"From how long?" asked Ajja sitting cross-legged at his priestly place, in-front of the horse, dropping few more crumbs of benzoin on to the glistening ember. It must have glimmered and liquidated those crumbs in no time, slowing the aroma into the air. There was a transmutation from one state to the other without any shy.

Visitors seemed to have got puzzled by the question. Is the 'how long' for fever or for the husband's unemployment? They appeared to arrive at a conclusion after a collective brood. The lady certainly considered it for fever and replied appealingly —

"From the past four days Saheb."

Ajja nodded his head gesturing them to sit down, and went on to prepare an amulet with a small paper and some pasty substance and locketed it to a black thread. They looked edgy and observed Ajja's deft hands diligently.

"Are you from Malur?"

"Yes."

Once the talisman was ready, she woke her child up to see the world. Ajja knotted it firmly in the defiant neck of that child. Wisps of loban were hitting their faces and inverted back to create small clouds that were supposed to precipitate the blessings on them. Ajja imparted the blessings of god by touching all of their heads with the feather bunch that I had propelled beside him. The gentleman bent forward to pay the obligatory honorarium, unaware of the oldman's ideals just like another visitor; Ajja's hand refusing it looked even more graceful. As though he forgot something of the essence, he plunged into his handbag to fish-out something, but ignored it on the spur of the moment and smiled at Ajja with an apologetic crimsoned face.

Then, they rose up to bid a gratuitous farewell; lady had the child on her shoulder and the gentleman many-things. Those disheveled and unbalanced souls leaving in the scorching sun had left me in a choke of sympathy. *Sympathy need not be a privilege of the wealthier; it is another word for the compassion, an essence of all sorts of life, the red of the blood, the white of the bones, the breath of life.* As they trudged on the walkway from the veranda till the main gate, cursed by the time, an unknown impulse drove me to perform something unexpected. I took out the paper and pencil from my pocket and wrote four double digit numbers and handed it over to Ajja. He took a glance at the chit and looked into my eyes thoughtfully, combing his sheeny beard gently with his fingers. Then he rose up to call out the couple, who were receding from the door frame.

"Hey maalik, come over here." The man turned back with a little trepidation. He got to his feet and paced back till the veranda with a question mark on his tanned face. His wife stood at the entrance under the shade of tamarind tree and kept staring at us with inquisitive eyes, cuddling her already slept baby.

Ajja presented the piece of paper and whispered something in his ears. The man looked a little thrilled at once and folded his hands with gratefulness before taking a leave. His eyes got a new glow and the lips attempted to break a smile; his feet were boosted up with a new vigor as he made his way to join his family.

"It's all his game, his moves unpredictable, unstoppable and inescapable like the births and deaths, like the winds and rains..." Ajja had his time again.

I walked till the gate to see them leave. Husband struggled to kick start his old, rusty, thirsty, sick motorbike, parked under tamarind tree; they seemed to have forgotten to ask one more amulet for it. His wife asked him something curiously, caressing the child's scalp on her shoulder, but he looked at the skyline and seemed to be in a hurry to generate a spark with his athletic kicks. As the bike started, exhaling the dark smoke and making the shriek sounds, woman mounted the pillion lithely comforting her extended life over the shoulder again. He waited for her consent to move, and in no time, the scooter sashayed and they faded away into the slopy bend flying off brown dust and dark smoke into the air.

It was all silent again, like the quiet after an unseasonal rain. Drongo, seated at its regular place, on a tender twig of the sacred fig, gauged at me with pride, steadying it's red-berry like eyes. I resumed my usual life — indulged into watering the saplings, organizing the stuff at sanctum, washing utensils after the meal, and so on. Ajja retreated back into his room, like a saint into his cave. We did not discuss anything of the visitors; still and all there was a thrill in me, a sense of accomplishment, a sense of contentment. It was more intense than my success in math class. I was compelled to play with the numbers for the rest of that afternoon, while Ajja kept himself weltered with his old scriptures and scribbling.

I probed into myself with the number-charts to find out that how did I arrive at those specific numbers. I couldn't arrive at any clue. The more conscious I grew and the more logical I became, they didn't just come out. 'One can even tame a tiger, but not the river' — I heard the muffled words of Ajja emanating from his study. When I played with them innocently, those elusive numbers, when I remained as unsullied and clear as a blue sky, out of the blue, they manifested like a rainbow. I attempted to go beyond the skies of my mind and failed miserably. They evaporated and faded soon like the dew drops even before I could attempt to comprehend the canvas, before could I reach its beginnings and ends, before could I fathom its means and origins.

*****

The yellows and pinks of mirabilis opened their arms and yearned for an embrace, sensing my presence, like a pet dog that wags his tail and gets excited on the arrival of his master. It was that dawn, my father was asleep on his charpoy, and his white shirt had an aura of lurid glow, as though he was bathed in the stream of liquid moon. I woke him up with a tap on his shoulder. There were two precincts he had to cross — the inebriation and the slumber. He looked at me flowering up a smile. His oily face glistened in the silvery moonlight. I whispered and shared him the slip with two numbers written over it; I also put a condition and took a promise from him — to bring all the bounty to home. He rubbed his eyes and gazed at me with a great veneration as though he was in front of a god. I peered in through the half opened door; mother seemed to be drowned in her fanciful dreams. I chose not to spoil her sleep and took the leave from the place surreptitiously.

The other night, I went near the home again and lurked outside, peeping through the gaps of bamboo wall. It's mother, seated before the flaming earth oven, delightful, glowing brighter than the golden sun, busy counting the money from two bundles with her radiant smile and saliva that wetted her thumb now and then. Father, seated on folded straw mat sipping his brandy in a steel glass, looked at her proudly. After a brief spell of silence, he broke the ice saying, "It's all his Leila, his own divine play." Mother lifted her head to acknowledge with a questioning countenance.

"Your son," he completed his sentence.

"I saw him talking to you in the dawn…" she replied.

"What are you planning to do with it?" he asked referring to the bundle of notes in her hands with his glass.

"Will buy four buffaloes," her nose ring glistered and the eye-brows almost touched the ears. Father took the last sip and had a laugh.

A bellow of rage mounted up and subsided in me like a hungry tide in the sea.

"You do whatever the hell you want," father said coldly. Wiping off a pearl of drink that was about to trinkle down from his dark lower lip.

Mother continued counting the notes in her own pace.

I broke into the home, propelled by an outrageous exasperation. Lights began flickering. "Avva, enough of all this. No more buffaloes please. We have got enough money to lead a decent life."

None of them paid any heed. Inebriated father, stretched down over the straw-mat. Mother began stirring the boiling rice with a wooden ladle, ignoring my presence. "Mother, I have earned lot of money now. I have roamed around the world. Have my own flat let's go and live there, the world is not just what you think. It's not just about buffaloes. It's wide and colorful; you should go out and see." I screamed my heart out. They don't even look at me. The fire in the oven aggravates, rice boils with the blisters bursting on its surface. Cradling the bundles of notes, mother keeps stirring with her same indifference.

It's another nightmare that freezes me in the bed. I brood on the extent of absurdity that life grows to. I relive the past but it doesn't mean that I should time travel and fix the things up. Well, what is there to fix? For me, It's all like a momentary swing that draws one from the sublime to puerile and vice-versa over the time.

I sit awake on bed, my fancy of happening to meet Swathi, in the midst of many faces of strollers make me feel even more stupid. After-all what is it for? What will I do if I get to meet her like that? It's merely a fancy with no substance, a honeycomb with no honey. As alien and remote as 'what if the god manifests in-front of you'. For a bohemian man like me, family and social utilities are theoretical and literary concepts. I have come to accept that I don't know how to love. Even if the clone of Swathi comes and proposes me for marriage, will I be able to espouse her? I don't think so. For me, the holidays, children's birthdays, solving their boyfriend issues, remembering the wedding date and all that utilitarian stuff is hornets' nest. However, I don't deny the fact that there are nights on which I craved for another flesh beside me merely to see me dying. Every time when I got exhausted with the mundane routine of nine to six, every time when I reached the end of rope, I did give a consideration for marriage. Soon, I realize that the very thought is a pretext and a mere escape from the vexation. That idea never journeyed in me for more than a night. I happen to see men and women in subways and markets who are synonymous to the words — traditional, religious, righteous, pious, disciplined, god-fearing, and moral; in precise they are the children of god, who have achieved the merit of entry to the heaven already. One even could doubt that gods and angels would envy such people for their austere karmic discipline. Whenever I come across such men, there is a flickering thought in me that burns and dies — *'one should lead an idealist and principled life. I am sullied and unholy for it already; no I am not, she is the one who lied about her relationship status. It's her karma but not mine. If needed, I can take a dip in Ganges, four or five times as per the traditions. But, all of them, those who pose like the divine creatures, are they really what they show up? Is the grass on the other shore is as green as it looks in the digital photograph?'* A suspicion defends the status quo.

I rise up from the bed and stand in front of the mirror in bathroom. I survey on my protein deficient grey hair, sharp massive nose, two pits of chicken pox on the right cheek and non-trimmed thick facial hair, on the forehead the traces of lines of fate written by the lord *Brahma* and now erased and rewritten by the man himself, it's him none other than, Lakshman Chalavadi, once a discarded, out casted, expelled, now a true son of India. I ingratiate myself.

There come two honks from the road beating my ear drum to howl me out. I open the curtain. It's the same chrome-yellow school van. Children of the apartment, freshly bathed, neatly cropped, perfumed, attired in immaculate, ironed uniform from head to toe, accompanied by the over-solicitude of their parents, say 'bye,' in unison while their respective mothers carrying sleepy eyes and disheveled hair yet with lipstick, and few fathers in fancy night dresses, stand at the opened gate and wave at them with pride, as though their children are heading to a space mission. I watch the spectacle from the lee of clothesline in the balcony, unclipping my clothes one after the other. I am none of them, I ruminate. Neither among those parents, nor among the children. I must be the only black sheep in the entire apartment. Suppose, I had a family, would I send off my children to school that way? I would have to pretend my every gesture; would have to re-stitch my whole being. I would have to act away my entire life. It doesn't seem as easy as paring my beard to adapt to the so called corporate culture.

I decide to put everything on paper before it evaporates. I wash my face; sit at my table with an empty paper and a lazy pen. Nothing comes out. It hides and sinks down to bury itself deep inside me, not as a corpse but as a seed. My pen behaves like a recalcitrant kid. *Can a mirabilis change its color if it is grown in the city? Can a bird sing a different song if it's caged in a concrete forest?* I write two lines and tear that paper off. Here again an intimidating blank page, challenges me like a glaring champion wrestler and provokes me to behave like the lost Robert de Niro of the Raging Bull all through the day. I realize it's late for my work. I rise up to take bath in my imaginary Ganges.

Chapter 13

Moonlight was so dazzling that I could see the trees so clear and could make out the lush verdancy of their leaves. The sharp shadows of the foliage had assumed their own existence and danced with no coyness for the rhythm of breeze. The full moon, which looked like the light of all the heavens, must have had a subtle reason that night to lend more glows to the effulgence that was borrowed from the sun.

The hill exuded its own perfume, and the breeze carried it everywhere like a hawker. The scent of its soul was refined out from the wild flowers like lantanas, night jasmines, spider lilies, mesquites, sacred datura and was blend with the aroma of *seethaphal*, *sapota*, lemon, guava, sheep perspiration and their droppings, burnt firewood and so on. Yet, the breeze seemed so fresh and elating without any worldly vein in it.

I was lying awake on my bed in veranda. Somewhere in the distance, sometimes from the south and sometimes from the east, a faint rattling sound of a tractor reached my ears, at times as faint as a flutter of an exquisite bird in the back of my mind. They must be ploughing, with a hope which was on par with the aridness of the very land that they harrowed. They seemed to carry it out all the night, till the sun and the moon meet up for a rendezvous. I heard Ajja reading aloud and speaking to himself alone in his room as he did now and then. After an hour or so, he fell silent and drifted into sleep. In the company of chaotic silence, my eyes went in a stroll about sacred fig, coco palm, *sapota*, cottony clouds and the alluring moon. Drongo must have slumbered in its nest along with its family on a warm bed of feathers. It's indiscernible that whether the goddess of sleep left me orphaned or it was me who discarded her. It must be both the ways for a reason. I contemplated on Gopal's accounts to deduce on how my mother and father would have taken the matter of my run off with the cold indifference.

It must be around sundown. Like the tired fowl, my mother and her other workmates, with stacks of green grass over their heads, plod on the green dyke. Perhaps, to chase-out the thoughts of weight over her head, and the arduous long-march till home, from the conscious frame of mind, or out of her impulse, one of mother's colleagues strikes a lighter conversation addressing avva in a taunting manner,

"I heard your son is settled in Dargah?"

And my mother, without letting out any sign of embarrassment or the regret, replies —

"Yes, that's the safest harbor and a comforting place for a boy like him."

The other lady must have tried to be nosy, and intervened in between for a sneer —

"It looks to me that he liked the food from Moula's house so much that he forgot his own home."

There should be an outburst of snigger followed by my mother's defending and befitting reply —

"One should be lucky enough to avail such privilege of on time food and peace of mind."

They must have sagged with discontent for failing to cloud my mother.

Though, I pacified my earnestness by supplying the questions and answers to the scene on my own, like filling colors to an outlined image. I urged myself to recollect the exact words in Gopal's narration that day.

To while away my quiet afternoon, I had set off for an exploration towards south petal of the hill. It was Gopal, who showed interest to come up till me leaving his herd behind, while I was picking up gooseberries. I was swept away by a surprise after realizing that it was him, whose afternoon folk concerts I enjoyed unpaid. A singing shepherd boy who competed with all the birds of the hill.

"It looks you are kind of liking here? Enjoying the place eh?"

Those matured pretensions of him had grown into his nature — direct to the point, picking up from the middle, avoiding the formal etiquettes of civil conversations that sounded hitting around the bushes. With a little jealousy towards his 'grownup' behavior, I preferred a short reply.

"Kind of…"

"So you won't be returning home?" he asked authoritatively as though a sibling of mine.

"Haven't thought of it yet."

"I think your parents are also least bothered about your exile," he said tightening up his slack towel around his head — his namesake turban.

"How do you know?" I asked with a fervid countenance.

"It's a fine morning, last week, that, I was passing by your house; your mother was busy washing the clothes, flowing a foamy stream across the road. There was a water-motor placed at the entrance of your shack. Your mother, while wringing out his shirt, asked your father 'what sort of a motor is it, what did you bring it for?' your father replied in his usual teasingly mirthful way — 'I have come to realize that a washing machine won't be sufficient for your wardrobe, so I have brought a three HP motor for your grand washing.' Your father is such a comic man," Gopal began laughing riotously. I attempted to mask my giggle with the curiosity, nonetheless I failed.

"'You are only good for such pompously ridiculous dialogues, why can't you go work somewhere and bring some money? Don't talk to me until you reclaim Kaali. It's all because of you that Lachya left home and settled in Dargah', your mother replied him furiously mentioning you."

I asked what did my father reply to that. Gopal continued enthusiastically —

"He said, 'he will be happy there instead of getting enslaved under you. It's because of your vexing him with petty works he left home in the midnight.'"

"And then?" I must have showed signs of earnestness on my face.

"Your father left the place, jumping his eyebrows at me. And the very next moment, Desai arrived to pick up that water-motor with a warning to your mother — 'Tell Malkaji, not to mess up with me. Or else you will have to leave the village forever'. It seems to me that, your father also knows Desai's secrets and that's the reason, he has a little soft corner towards your father. I just surmise it, I am not sure of it though. I like your father's wit, he always speaks like beating with a stone tied up in a towel, you feel it hard inside but it looks like a mere cloth to others outside," Gopal grew exuberant while speaking of my father.

Even in the past, he always succeeded in tempting me with the word 'secret', but I avoided the conversation tagging it unnecessary. I got myself convinced that, the time is ripe for it now and posed him the question,

"What is the secret that you know about Desai?"

He began to throw a mischievous smile colored with a sense of pride of his possession of secret, "Let it go, why simply discuss it…" he spoke thoughtfully like an elder, playing with the knot on his rope. I gazed at him with no expectations.

So he continued, "You should keep it to yourself and never utter a word of it to anyone. I am revealing it to you only because you are an insider for me," I nodded obediently expecting the pulpy part, "one afternoon, while I was at the grazing by the northern hedge of his farm with my black and white herd, I felt thirsty. Out of no choice, with an empty bottle in hand, I sauntered towards his shed through the shoulder-high maze. I am always confident about my herd, and trust in their discipline, but except those interns of that midwife. All of them do not move an inch in my absence you know. Sorry, I forgot where I was. Yes, as I approached the shed, I sensed something strange; I heard few noises coming out from his shed. I paused abruptly and tried to tune my listening pricking my ears, but the noises were quiet. Anyways, I wanted to take the u-turn for the sake of everyone's good, but my thirst you know? I dared to push myself further and to peep in slowly from the wide gap of the rusty broken door. That's it, I was met with such a scene that I had never witnessed in my life before. There were two nude figures on the bed. And then I realized that it was Desai making love with Yelli, sleeping over her. He was drowned totally between the pumpkin sized breasts of her...forget it," he took a respite with a sigh and pretense of shy, surveying my face for the clues of astonishment, and then continued —

"I had seen Yelli roaming in their farm several times with a pretext of collecting hay, firewood and things of that sort. But had not imagined what I witnessed in day light. Somehow, he seems to have got to know that I have seen him with her. He asked me to keep it with me and never utter a word of it to anyone. I revealed it only to you, as I believe that you are a trustworthy man." He looked into my eyes solemnly with a relief and searched for signs of shock and surprise.

It took me a while to recall the face of Yelli that Gopal had mentioned. She was a vagabond whose house was located near our school. I had seen her dipsomaniac husband declaring — 'He is not my son, He is not my son,' to his own son in public standing near *Dharmashale*.

As the day drew on, Gopal made many revelations that could place me on a swing of shockers.

As per Gopal, it was my father who provoked Chennappa for an adventure with him. Father was the mastermind, who had plotted a robbery at a governmental premise. He waited outside the Panchayat office propelling Chennappa inside to rob the place. Chennappa grabbed everything that came to his hands in a haste — calculator, two drinking glasses, microphone, a foldable chair, paper weight, some bucks from the drawer and at last even a wall portrait of MK Gandhi! They took all of loot to national highway and waited there for the stranger trucks to sell them off for any price as they did every-time. Gopal, even imparted the accounts of how my father with pride verbalized his feat after getting drunk in the evening.

"He bought everything, every single smallest of the things, but refused to accept that photo, the photo of Mahatma, he refused to buy. Does he know who Mahatma is? Well I pity on this country. Times are changed. It's no country for the martyrs. It's no country for the Mahatmas. They never offered him a space in their hearts but on their walls, and that's it. He kept hanging on the walls bathed in dust behind whom the lizards made their home. They will soon eliminate him from the currency notes, from the texts, from the squares and even from the walls. I can give it in writing, tomorrow, while they recheck what all is missing, they will list down every single thing but the photo of him. It's because, they have not given a space for him in hearts but on walls…"

Since the truck driver rejected to buy the portrait of Gandhi, they carried it back till the cross road near railway station and they hung it onto a roadside electric pole. So, all the passersby smile at Gandhi and he acknowledges them back.

As per Gopal, there was yet another incident in which the duo had managed to purloin the money-box and the metal feet of lord hanuman from the temple in the dead of a night. The way sculptor sees a potential masterpiece hidden in a wild rock, my father saw the victim commodities. Small or big, humanly or godly it never seemed to matter.

"Your father, goes and stands before the grand old man of the village Sharan Gowda, and speaks hilariously — 'Sir, it's because of the men like you, the earth is still getting to have rains. Those were the times sir, when you rode the seven-feet horse and ruled this village like a king. There are no morals left now; boys, who are not even the size of a bottle, began drinking and chewing gutka. Girls are running away to cities with strangers, ladies don't want to work but rest all the time watching tv. If nobody wants to work but rest all the time, how can we survive? None of the farmers want their sons to be farmers sir. We are heading towards very bad times. People have stooped so low that they began stealing god's feet and Gandhi's photo. Just imagine sir...' After this monologue, your father secretly opens the weary betel-nut pouch of old man, placed near his feet and snips the twenty rupees note and takes leave folding his hands. The best part is, Sharan Gowda, lost his hearing senses years ago and his eyes also barely see. Your father is such a funny man,' Gopal laughed again uproariously.

I had seen Sharan Gowda, many a times; a grand old man who wore thick glasses with a broken frame on his capsicum-like nose and gazed at the inner horizons bearing eyes wide open, like the luminescent candles and smiled with the inner lips. His bulged green veins all over the body and the senile solemnness made him a man to be remembered. He sat on the *pyol* of an old, now defunct cooperative society office right opposite to his house like a hoary idol of a forgotten god. Everybody in the village treated him with much respect and reverence. When Rani had got married; the couple had to take his blessings before heading to the temple.

I muddled in a deep confusion probing about the motives of my father behind his contemptible crimes like theft of public property. I had come to believe that Chennappa being an insane tramp, would not vent into such adventures on his own, it was father who used him like a sidekick, in-fact like a puppet. It is always proven to be an easier task to shift the responsibilities and culpabilities on to the shoulders of an unhinged man. And even the societies are used to presume the petty crimes for the deranged.

I had asked Gopal for his opinion on the reasons of my father's thievery and he had an instant and crisp response ready for it — "To drink; to drink their throat-full. And to play matka, they can't live without them and they can't die without them," as I gaped at him like another innocent sheep in his herd, he continued in a concerned voice — "he sold your Kaali to Desai's relatives for a very trifling price. All felt bad for your mother."

I remember how hard was the struggle, to shut my eyes and to escape from the resonance of moving images shaped by Gopal's nonplusing disclosures. Bye and large, the encounter with Gopal was a fortunate stroke of serendipity. Happening to come across him accidentally was like discovering a hidden cave in the hill, a cave with many ears and eyes. Finally, there had to be an agreement between me and the sleep. The night fell like an incomplete episode of life. The hill must have breathed and its heart must have beated. Clouds must have journeyed like a hungry herd into the wild, moon must have grown old in my absence bearing the furrows carved by time. I must have sprouted in my own absence, like a lonely seed at the base of an ancient well. It was then, a bizarre event transpired.

A lush-green-plane stretched till the skyline and meandered towards the infinity, in which an old man with the ethereal facial hair and a turquoise colored turban, rode on a white horse, in the slow motion, swooped along my left. Perhaps, I was on a horse too, a black or a brown one, rising and swooping at my own pace. His profile moved up and down, blocking and unblocking the sun as he rode past me.

In the same lumbering pace he turned to smile and beckon at me. His radiant visage and the angelic aura managed to hypnotize me in no time, even before my perception could inscribe his image. There was no way that I could escape that enthralling magnetic pull. My heart thudded with a wild excitement and I made every effort to gallop. Withal, I didn't move an inch. He turned again to call me up, reining his stallion with his left hand, wearing the same decorous smile. I seemed helpless being trapped in the monstrous clutches of the gravity. I began to suspect, if the horse that I rode was even alive. He receded too far and faded in the horizon into the green. I stood there like a statue, benumbed and perplexed, staring at the intimidatingly desolate path.

The fine dust on the tender leaves of the new saplings was being sluiced out by the silver drops as I watered the nursery. The same face that seemed unusually intimate in the dream, manifested in my mind and the scene was replayed in the same vividness. Eventually, I realized that it's the same portrait that I had watched all the day. The portrait of a nameless Sufi saint that Ajja called his Guru, which was hand drawn by himself and was water colored. Nonetheless, he admitted many a times that he drew it post the departure of his Guru. So the portrait should be the result of his imagination. There is surely a striking similarity in the texture of memories and the grains of dreams.

Chapter 14

I squinted my eyes to follow the pace of an unknown motorcycle that sped away like a guided missile along the skyline and disappeared beyond the spire of railway station leaving the trails of dark smoke behind. "He must be a man with an iron heart," I said within. *Brave men take risks, but they make sure that those risks are well weighed and meticulously gauged. They don't drive the life itself into a grave risk.* The copper pot was full till the rim by then and even overflowed wetting my bare feet. The excess water had taken their course towards the huge trunk of the tamarind tree that stood like a green brolly to create a parking space for the visitors' vehicles before Dargah. A chewed up, capsule-like metallic pendant looped into a faded black thread shone bright in the water course. It must be an old amulet belonged to the sick baby of the struggling couple who had visited us recently. I lifted the pot spryly on-to my right shoulder and carried it into the yard crouching a little at the door-less doorway. The wind seemed to had got new spirits and the youthful chirp of birds sounded like their song of freedom. Drongo wasn't spotted at its habitual place.

The mornings at the summit are always ceremonial in their own ways. Somewhere near, in one of the surrounding villages, in the vicinity, there must be a wedding going on. A troupe of three *shehnais* and a pair of battered drums that are tied to the waist of the drummer (which look like *tabla* and sound like *nagara*) were creating the music that could call upon the angels to descend for a moment. The band seemed to know only two songs, one for the marriage and the other for the death. At the summit, though it sounded like a piece of music from a forgotten dream, its nostalgic euphony could evoke hundreds of images in my mind. Whenever the leading *shehnai* reached its pinnacle, a sort of falsetto, it

reminded me of a question that stayed with me for a long time —
why do they play the music in weddings? Certainly to draw the
attention of neighborhood; it is said to be auspicious as it impresses
the angels and gods and compels them to wish the couple; it
generates positive vibrations; reminds the bride and groom every
single moment that they are going through something
transcendental and so on, were the answers that I collated from
different sources of my thought process. But what I favored the
most was that, such live music creates a sense of mood to hook
everyone into one common goal and to keep things going on. I
have seen relatives with differences, patching up quickly and
embracing each other as though nothing happened — the mood
for that moment of goodness and benevolence is created by this
music — 'Don't cry now, don't you hear the *shehnai*? It's the
wedding day today; one should never shed tears'. All through the
event, from beginning till the end, it seems to work as an
undercurrent, which places everyone in a cheerful, attentive and a
sort of hypnotic trance. I seem to had experienced such a state
during Rani's nuptials. As I stood by an electric pole near my house
and observed the ceremony closely, I was strangely convinced that,
it was the music, which contained all the intoxicated madness of
my father, selfishness of my mother, innocence of the bride and
groom and the ignorance of the people around. Every-time, when
the music was stopped, people used to grow conscious and look
awkwardly at each other's eyes, including the bride and groom.
Rani, who accompanied me to all the good hells and bad heavens,
now stood apart and looked like a stranger draped in a *saree* and
her own self. Before the music could cease in me, before the scent
of *sambhar* from the feast evaporated, she had left us, as though
she had gone out to school or to the play. She had left us to a far-
away town. A sense of emptiness had invaded me to keep me awake
for several nights brooding on how vulnerable is the life with

regards to the parting from someone integral with the self; as easy as a leaf falling off from the tree.

Whether one is brave or coward, leaving the house at some juncture of life is a mandatory course of action for the women of this land; perhaps, to the women of all the lands. It appears to me that, this is the reason behind naming all the rivers after women — Ganga, Yamuna, Cauvery, Godavari and so on. They are to flow in their own course and keep assimilating the life in whatever manner it stretches on their way. They are to swell up and shrink down in the gravels of time.

That night, when the mother had spoken of Rani giving birth to babies sooner or later, the very thought of it froze me benumbed and I couldn't shut my eyes the whole night. I appear to had established that it was a painful and macabre phenomena to give birth to a new life. Creation is equally painful and beautiful. I had witnessed Kaali giving birth to Dyami with tears in her eyes — first the ball of a slimy substance dangling out from the vagina for some time like a jelly pendulum and then the yellow hooves appeared followed by the face of the calf. But the incident that had left a dreadful impression on me was the death of Shaila. A cursed flower; that is what comes to my mind whenever an image of her passes before my inner eye. She was neither a bud nor a flower, neither a girl nor a lady; she was simply Shaila, merely elder by a year to Rani. "After-all an intern, a student, she came out like a devil in apron, and crisscrossed the pregnant belly with a merciless scissor. And the blood gushed out like a frenzied river and never ceased to flow. How could they allow probationers to play with the tender lives? Outrageous. Our people shouldn't have chosen that hospital run by unscrupulous amateurs." Those were the words rolled on the streets as Shaila turned into ashes. Her bruised boy will grow up someday to question the world holding its collars for its sins and wickedness.

I brooded till the stream of my thoughts had overtaken the rider of the disappeared motorcycle.

Women are born adventurous and men are born for adventures.

Ajja had gone on an errand around the summit and kept himself mettlesome collecting the herbs to prepare his peculiar medicines for our once-in-the-blue-moon visitors. He had a line of earthen pots and containers in the sanctum, in which he preserved powders of dry leaves and other ingredients like acacia-gum and the wax of honeycomb that smelled like the fossils of Harappan civilization —a dying man's obsession to save the lives of unknowns. I went up to him after my routine rituals — sweeping the veranda and watering the plants. With the backdrop of the open lands and endless sky, he looked like a foreigner to me, even homuncular and fragile. His walking stick groaned and flailed for the tenacity of his left hand. He was busy plucking out ripe lemons, fragrant and lustrous canary-yellow. An angry gust of the wind disturbing the fine dust, revealed his emaciated frame, as his lose attire stuck to his bones. His typical ankle-length *lungi* and the bone-white *jubba* struggled hard to escape and fly away, even before the bird in his rib cage did. That fleecy facial hair of him streamed in all the directions; resisted and surrendered to the wind.

"We should pluck them, before they fall down. They are old; they are done with growing and evolving. They are just a burden to the tree now. We should pluck them out, before they fall down. We should make a way out for the green ones. To wither and decay is also a phase of evolution, do you see it?" he spoke, looking at my shadow again sensing my presence, in his characteristic cryptic way with the customary repeated remarks.

I wanted to ask the question that pestered like a mosquito in my mind. *Express your heart amidst the nature, the god's ultimate expression.* That's what I believed in.

"Ajja, what is that you read every night? I hear you murmur like a pigeon." He bursted into a sidesplitting guffaw with short pauses for momentary cough. His brilliant infantile laugh stood on par with the best expressions of nature, likely of those ripe lemons and the dancing poppies.

"It's an empty book that I read! Let me tell you a secret. All should attempt to read an empty book, every so often. It might sound ludicrous for you, isn't it? You might want to ask, how to read and what to read from an empty book. It's quite possible. All that I read is from blank pages. You can try it on your own as well. What can you read when an entire page is full with emptiness? It's all emptiness alone that you can gauge on and nothing else. It's a great method to lustrate the sanctum of your heart. Divine thoughts born there like the flowers of heaven and their fragrance pervades your sanctum like that of a sublime *loban*. Peersab always used to tell me this. On a fine day, I had asked him of how he could compose and sing the folk-songs spontaneously like an act of nature, for that, he had revealed me this exercise. When there is nothing that you are taking in, all that's left is to give out."

It sounded absurd and made me curious at the same time. Who is *Peersab*? I had never attempted reading an empty book. At the edge of my consciousness there was a thought that peeped in like a cricket — Ajja must be going through his senile madness.

Since couple of nights, there were a series of eerie internal monologues emanated out from his room, part clear and part muffled. I surmised that it must be the result of senescent schizophrenic auditory illusions; in other words, a pure madness. On one occasion, I even took the courage to sidle till his door and stole a glance at him. Found him on his bed with the eyebrows lifted and forehead wrinkled, busy reading out from an anonymous book — a title-less volume. All that he uttered seemed to be a sort of vague philosophical dangling sentences, self-reflection and criticisms about human condition. As long as he murmured, a part of my heart felt relieved. The silence from his room scared me more than his deliration. The very notion of me, going and standing at his bed, finding him breathless and then forcing a cry or be frightened of his dead-body or to merely hoist the flag and leave the place informing his family, placed me on tenterhooks at times.

That night, I must have made my bed a little closer to his door, with an idea to eavesdrop on his secret rendezvous which I thought was the corollary of senile dementia. My eyes took refuge in gazing at the patterns of bamboos in the ceiling for a while. It was all dark around. Orange light was seeped out from the edges of the door of his room. Though the door was closed, there was never a practice of latching it. I had pricked my ears for the show to begin, it was then an idea fell upon me from the roof like a Newton's apple. I prepared myself to jot down his soliloquy with a pencil and a notebook. I waited earnestly like a photographer who waits for a bird to flutter to capture the action, to sculpt in the time.

How far can you go,

riding a wooden horse?

will it carry you till the gate

forget of changing your fate.

There should be a little ball of phlegm obstructing his words, he cleared it off with a thunderous cough and continued —

never it lets you fall

nor it aids you rise

breathless and zestless

strainless and thirst-less,

His words quivered as they rolled out. My pencil and paper seemed more attentive than me, scribbled them with a fervor of catching the slithery fish into the basket. I had lost my presence for a moment even to realize that I was placed out of the realms of time and space.

callous to the pulse

heartless to the pain

no shine in the muscles

no ups or the downs

all it conjures is a solipsistic sound

tuk tuk tuk tuk, deceives your will

but will never carry you

up to the hill

what good is it to rest in the grave

before tasting the nectar of the brave

never ride a wooden horse

my comrade, never...

There sprung a sense of turmoil in me, like a hundred swords parrying at once in the mind. Though my hand kept writing to give in after a while, my jejune mind was compelled to visualize the horse in the sanctum — whole of that beautiful wooden sculpture, and questioned Ajja's mysterious motives of disparaging it with his madness. At times I did even presume that he must be jealous of his Guru, for the matter of not possessing a magnificent horse like his master did.

I don't remember whether he went on further with his stream of strange words or it was me who ceased to note them down. All I can assure is, the night drew on in an absurd and nostalgic adornment. The faint fragrance of the hill and the words of Ajja, had placed me on a surreal drive. A deep whistle of the early-morning train corroborated the departure of the night towards the unknown.

Chapter 15

As I rush into the staircase avoiding the elevator that was free and appealing for a lift, opening its wide arms to embrace its long lost friend, the security calls me up,

"Sir...Laxman Sir..."

Rather going back till his cabin, I choose to wait at the stairway. He trots till me with a sort of inquisitive grin. I stand pretending to be in a hurry, fidgeting with the device in hand, scrolling it up and down.

"Sir it's from three days that I tried to chase you,"

"Chase me?"

"I meant to say, I tried to meet and have a word with you,"

"So what is it about?"

"You have got a parcel…"

There is a relief of getting down from a nightmarish roller-coaster. He scuttles back to his cabin to fetch it.

"By any chance, was it you who knocked at my door?"(*In the fit of pique, I would have committed a blunder* — I bite my tongue in embarrassment) "By any chance, did you knock at my door, yesterday night?" I want to ask this rephrased question, but I don't.

It's a light carton box that demands all the five fingers to clasp it. He attempts to look into my eyes with a sly. I inch away from the place with the same pretense — busy with the device, anticipating the source of the received package as there is no return address stated on it.

It's not new with him. In the past when I followed her, though with the ample gaps of five to ten minutes, to and from the morning walks, he stared at me wily as though I was flirting his own wife. That strange envy, that inquisition, that snooping through those sleek cabins are the fundamental traits of any seasonal security guard in our country. Just like any other blue-collar construction laborer, he too an uncouth, unlettered migrant bird from the north. It's nothing other than one's sheer ignorance to expect from him, the dignity and grace of an English porter. Only way to shut his mouth is to speak to him in English, he doesn't know the native language nor English. He retreats his nose with "Yess sir, thenks sir." I mollify my mind and succeed in propitiating it with the sacrifice of his last bit of honor, before unlocking the door.

A thought that dawns over the horizon, recedes in the same speed — *I don't think they can blow me up with a postal bomb.* As I saunter into the room, soon after I rest the mysterious box on the teapoy, my feet make their way towards the window, like a ritual which they are obliged to follow. There is no one. Not even a dog.

I unearth the mystery, stripping it one layer after the other, like venting to reach the heart of a gypsy girl. My curiosity swells up with its heaviness and my hands lose no time. It's an antique alarm clock, mounted on the back of a horse. Yes, a wooden horse! A well carved, lustrous horse with the glossy body that hefted the time over its back; a tour-de-force of an anonymous virtuoso.

I stretch myself on the bed, place it on my side table and stare at it for no reason with a strange mindfulness. *It's blatantly metaphoric* — says my heart. I give a thought to fling it into an unreachable corner in the shelf, but I let it stand — a memento, a testimonial of my brazen fiasco.

There are some whispering noises from the passageway. It must be of the tricycle of boy from last door in the corridor. His granny must be supervising his play. He plays with the motion, with the velocity, with the drift; his mind swoops up and down as he cycles down the way. *Motion is the fundamental nature. The stagnation stinks. You molder and crumble in an eternal torpor.* Who says to whom? Within me is again a conundrum. The horse stares at me, while the time on its back doesn't pay any heed to anything. Time is a merciless monster and a winsome flower at the same time. It's the heart-beat of the existence that never stops. In the name of evolution it has swallowed up many Laxmans like me. I follow the clock ticks, and attempt to fraction the second after second.

It's all dark; the voices are hushed in the corridor. I barely see the hands now. Light is consumed by the time. It moves flagrantly, like a snake creeping in your back. How could one hold it? I rise up to turn on the lights.

After the visit of the couple with an ailing child, in the matter of few days, we had several more pilgrims I suppose. As for me, I remained obscured for a profound purpose, behind the ornate green hangings, behind all the scenes at the sanctum, almost like a god whom they say is behind everything.

"Saheb I have come from far, we fell short with the money for my daughter's marriage. I have to buy some gold for the groom; else the marriage will be called off. We have already distributed wedding cards to all of our relatives. Please bless us and show us some way Saheb. If everything goes well, I shall buy some metal sheets to make some shelter in the front-yard of Dargah. We have surrendered to you and see no other way but you Saheb." He seemed to had placed forward his daughter's wedding card to testify his appealing implores.

The man hid his weaker being behind a thick greying moustache and tanned visage. Like those who hide behind the dark glasses — daylight cowards. Anybody could make out that he gambled with the rain and fed the crops with his sweat. He had a green tiny diary in his worn-out shirt pocket, may be to keep a note of transactions that he made, pertaining to the farm activities and perhaps for the marriage itself. His hair was colored with the brown dust and the fly hay had stuck there between the lose knots; these factors of his prosopography were certainly reiterating the fact that he was a son of soil.

I experienced a kind of thrill, for watching people through the gaps and slits from the anonymity. We had curtained either sides of the horse with green hangings in such a way that it sailed our mission smoothly. Visitors could only see the protruding face of the stallion from a sort of swaying wall and nothing else. This experience compelled me to realize on why barber Babu in our village desperately fancied for one-way glass and finally got it installed at his saloon. He could watch on everyone in the bazar street but nobody could see him back. All they saw were their own reflections on the mysterious modern looking dark opaque glass and behind that stood the master twirling his weapons around the heads of his unvarying clienteles. 'Time has changed, we have to adapt to that', he used to say. Often times, I essayed to understand what did he mean by his philosophical remark - 'Time has changed', and I could never assimilate how and where is it changed. Perhaps he must have meant that the people and their perspectives are changed over the time. *Time changes everything except itself.*

"It's not me that who blesses you, but him," Ajja pointed his hand towards the statue with a conspiratorial look. I could sense what he meant — 'it's him behind the curtain who could help you' and that 'him' could be the god or Laxman. After another round of *loban*, wafts of smoke pervaded the entire sanctum holifying all the ants, flies, mosquitoes, caterpillars and what not.

"Where are you from?" Ajja asked humbly with a partial smile.

"Kirsur, Saheb," the man replied instantly, presuming that his entreaties must have worked.

"You can pray wholeheartedly to the lord, he will surely help you," said Ajja assuring an unknown god's mercy.

I got the nod of Ajja and wrote four numbers in a piece of paper and slid it till where it's reachable to his hand.

As the visitor was all alone, Ajja opted to impart the instructions in a lower voice avoiding an intimacy of whispering in the ears that he usually did.

"There are three conditions for this to work, you should never speak about it to anyone, you should never tell a fib in the shrine, and you should never come back here with such request."

"As you say Saheb," the man nodded obediently for the secret commands and accepted the paper like a boon from god, pressed it to his eyes and joined his hands to Ajja before leaving the place. As he walked out from the sanctum into the silvery sun, it looked like he had got new wings all of a sudden.

It appears to me that, we create conscious memories for the deeds that we carry out whole heartedly with a sheer purpose. Memories of first love remain forever like the scar of a vaccine on shoulder, only because it blossoms out devoutly like an eternal flower and evolves with us in time. I don't agree to her remarks that the 'memories are fiction' but for me, they are evolved impressions of life. They are the scars on the skin of mind that expand, condense and wrinkle with the cells, with the time. As far as I remember, we had two more guests that day.

"Saheb, my brother has seized patrimonial share of my land from me. Instead of wrangling with him all my life, I have decided to establish a Gristmill business; I have shortage of some money, kindly help me. If all goes well, I will donate a real horse to this Dargah."

I felt I had seen this man somewhere, might be at the weekly bazaar, or in the village fair, or with the sand laborers near water-tank. He had cat eyes and four and a half fingers in the right hand; a deep scar on one of his temple proved the fact that he had been adventurous all through his life.

Ajja's hand went for the loban — a gesture to say, we are good to give him the right numbers. I wrote four numbers with a great vehemence and placed the chit on the floor, near Ajja. The pilgrim was imparted with the terms and conditions in a whisper. If there was anything that thrilled me the most was his remark — 'I shall donate a real horse to Dargah'. It generated a sparkle of novelty in my mind, an unknown joy for the mind's eye, like an omen from a forgotten life. Nonetheless, Ajja's imperturbation for his offer placed me in a complicated maze.

The last man to visit us that day was from the village Tarnal. He didn't seem honest to Ajja. Thus, we furnished him with the chit of false numbers.

"Saheb, I am suffering in the swirl of debts, please help me," that man had pleaded.

"Why did you make loans?"

"I burnt my hands ignorantly in some business Saheb."

Ajja had signaled me with a no, without further enquiries. No matter how hard that I tried to catch a glimpse at his face, I was blocked by the swaying green hangings. Nonetheless, I heard his voice clearly; a spurious and synthetic voice, waning with disappointment in the dying light of the sunset.

I think it was the same night or the other that as soon as the mumble of Ajja began, I went closer to the door and unrolled my straw-mat mutely to make my bed. My pencil and the notebook had grown voyeuristic and extremely brazen to jot down the bleak musings of a desolate old man.

"You are making the wrong move," his voice echoed, followed by a haunting silence of several seconds. For a moment I thought that he got to know about my earwigging outside, and hence closed my eyes.

"Who is judging? That something is right or wrong? To make a grand right move, I am bound to make few wrong moves. So then, to all its intents and purposes, how will it be a wrong move?" he continued after a cough, "but... but behind that big right move, the shadows of the smaller wrong moves will hound like ghosts. You can never build a right home with wrong bricks," he took a deep breath before giggling to himself and continued, "here the question itself is wrong and the answers too. Calling something wrong is also wrong in first place." There was a brief pause and then a series of coughs.

"Cross the forest

of rights and wrongs

by riding your white horse.

You have the earth if you fall

You have the skies if you don't

What do you have, if you don't ride at all?

Not even the manure of the horse,"

Ajja laughed again coughing in the middle, so much so that one would get confused whether it was a cough or his laugh.

*****

After a week or so, I woke up to a miracle in the morning. Though the poets proclaim that every morning is a miracle, on that specific sunrise I had to rub my eyes and pinch myself, to believe that whatever I was witnessing was real. A young, radiant milk-white stallion manifested in the leftward front-yard, facing the sun under the high roofed open shed (of metal sheets which was built the previous day with an idea to pile up any material donations to the shrine). I was enthralled by the look of new guest to Dargah. It's ethereal body, the streaming mane, those enchanting blue-pearl like eyes and the handsome gait seemed illusory at the first sight.

Ajja named it Sumeru.

It seems to me that I had asked Ajja, about the motives behind naming it 'Sumeru' and the meaning of that very word. He had replied, "It's an endless mountain that every human wants to ascend in their lives." All I was heard of were few mountains in geography class of the likes of Mount Everest and Mount Abu apart from the very hill that I dwelled in, but had never come across something called Mount Sumeru. Ajja must have expounded more about the mysterious mountain. Nevertheless, my memory has discarded all those details and settled with one distilled idea — Sumeru is a sort of mythical mountain.

I took Sumeru for the grazing that eventide along with Ajja. At first, as I paced behind that heavenly beast, I was troubled by a thought that reckoned it all to be a grand illusion. However, looking at Ajja's serine countenance, I forced myself to believe that it's all natural in life. He celebrated the silence all through our walk and began his herbalism as we reached the small stretch of farm at the north brow of the hill, belonged to Dargah.

"How do you gauge and conclude that someone is genuine and the other is not? How do you decide on whom to give the right numbers?" I asked Ajja to strike a conversation.

"We can determine by looking at their eyes. The guy who claimed he should be helped for his state of 'swirl of debts' wasn't clear in his motives, his words were vague, he was nervous, he was lying. At his age, all he could have done in life is playing cards and chasing ponytails." He dumped his collection of leaves and fruits into a piece of checkered cloth spread on ground in the lee of a bush.

Sumeru, began his browsing in the new landscape, that waited for him like an incomplete painting.

"What I wonder is, how come no one asked that, why four numbers are given from which only one will be correct?"

Ajja broke into a chuckle, plucking the leaves of a creeper that was spread evenly on a huge boulder.

"They might have understood that the message is clear: don't be too greedy at once."

On the very first instance when an unknown impulse drove me to the bailiwick of prognostication i.e. the practice of sharing the numbers, I began a tradition of distributing four numbers to each person, though I knew that only one is correct among them. Why so? I had not the least idea, all together a fortuitous encounter. It was later found out to be the desired way of doing such stuff! When the multiple numbers are shared, one has to divide the sum and wager, hence no extremities.

Looking at Sumeru, the next question propped up on the horizon.

"Why was this place named after White-Horse-Dargah?"

"I am not sure; it was there even before my coming here. Peersab must have thought that, if the Dargah is named after an animal, people from all the religions and castes could come. And moreover, Peersab's horse was also white. Now, it is a strange coincidence that the white-horse has come again to do the real justice for the name of Dargah."

The morning on which I ascended the hill for the first time, the foremost thing that I was compelled to behold were the elephantine letters written in white paint on a massive boulder situated at a view point that read, 'White Horse Dargah' with a deformed arrow mark at the end. I had then presumed that there could be a white-horse in it and hence the name. However, it was a rude awakening for me to discover that the white-horse referred in the sign board turned out to be the wooden sculpture of the horse that stood in the shrine. The arrival of the real horse certainly brought an air of life and charm to the hitherto desolate Dargah.

Like a river that swells up by the season, gradually, the number of pilgrims to the shrine began flourishing. In place of three, there were six or eight visitors per day. All were from different villages located around the hill. Few sought for god's mercy and the rest merely counted on the blessing, the way it descends upon. Sparked by the whispers from ear to ear, there was smoke rising up evidently from the concealed fire. The smoke that could create the humongous clouds and precipitate on the hill like never before.

Chapter 16

I was all alone with Sumeru in the western petal of the hill, where there spread the patches of sparse grass, though not lush green or not wholly yellow, but like my thoughts right now — light lime. I had collected few unripe *Seethaphals* from the young trees. They were of a kind that turn dark and wither away when they still used to be youthful. What good is it to die young in the tree? I flung them one by one, in a hope to send them across the foot of the hill. Nevertheless, all of them failed to escape. It's hard to say that it's due to lack of my force or their will.

The wild stillness around ignited a camouflaged impulse in me; an instinct of every man, a profound urge of every fledgling boy — to ride; a flare of desire to mount Sumeru.

I had an experience of riding Kaali, though it was only once, it still merits to be counted for an experience. One has to be a man to mount a horse. My fancy of riding Sumeru seemed to have stemmed out from a trunk with many roots. "If you ride, you have the sky, If you fall, you have the earth." Ajja's soliloquy had many remarks that coaxed me to pursue the thought at subconscious level. 'Go, give it a try. Come on, go for it', the stillness whispered persuasively like a friend from past life. Sumeru seemed to be aware of my touches well. Those cells under the shiny fur seemed to have registered the scintillas of my affectionate fondles as there was already a sort of amiability and warmth between us. An unparalleled similitude, stood like a wall around our combined solitude. In other words, we were the twins of life propelled into the wilderness by the conspiracy of time. I manufactured the courage out of my credence and began loosening the sideline hobble nimbly at the hind hoof. However, I was thwarted by a rattling apprehension and dreadful anxiety. My hands left the hobble at that, fastening it as it was before. I chose to step back and watch him grazing. His enigmatic eyes looked as though they read all of my thoughts. The mud road along the plane convinced and reminded me that the moment is well ripened for my experiment. 'Even if you fall down, there is no one to snigger at you, there are no gravels to break your forearm' — cajoled the manly version of me.

Many moons ago, during the festival of *Panchami*, Rani was playing with the tree swing, strung to a leaning branch of a tamarind try near our shack. She soared and swooped rhythmically standing on the wooden swing seat. In her blue skirt, at times she looked like a like a peacock in its flight. As she refused to offer me a chance to play, I had shaken the swing savagely from behind and had lifted it up till her feet slipped from the seat. She plummeted on to the ground like the heavy branch of a tree and her right forearm was hit to a sharp edge of the stone and was broken appallingly to become a partial L-shape. She yelped and howled like she was about to die. Her breath was caught for long in the middle of her gasp and her pain flowed all through her body warmer than her blood. I had got shivers and was unstrung by the mishap. It was all fixed up later after the treatment and apt medication in the government hospital. She hung her hand wrapped in plaster of Paris, to her neck for few days. 'To fall down, is to break your forearm' was the notion I had in my mind.

Since the ground was even and stone-free, I considered the thought again to mount, and gave a try without touching the hobble; clutching its withers tightly, I jumped-over to mount. As though it was prodded by a high-voltage electric wire, it flung me suddenly into the air and attempted a kick at me with the hindquarters. I found myself in the pit of misery as my elbow was scarred like a cat's painting and the blood was about to take the shapes of drops on surface. *When you fall from a horse, you don't fall in the middle of the road.* I applied my own saliva and tried to cool the wound. As for the horse, it grazed typically with the profound indifference, as though nothing had happened at all. Did I cry? It's hard to recollect, but I must have developed a deep contempt towards the horse. I whipped and drove it down the hill. For what? I still have no idea; to punish it for its disloyalty? Or to loosen its limbs up a little? Benumbed by the disillusionment, I trailed down mechanically like a captured war prisoner frogmarched by the sheer meaninglessness.

At the end of our descent, I left it at the foot of the hill to resume its scraping and sauntered towards the main-road. For what? It's an unknown impulse again. There seems to be an immediacy, when we happen to come across the rivers, hills, lakes, thickets and the meandering main roads, one wants to go there and witness with an intimacy.

"Ahh…" exclaimed I gaping at the portrait of Gandhi hanging serenely to the electric pole. I stood confounded for a while. Every year on his birthday, we all woke up before the sun and attired in spick-and-span milk-white uniforms and hoisted flags and sang songs. "Happiness is when what you think, what you say, and what you do are in harmony," there used to be speeches by the compatriot students and 'distinguished guests'. Swathi had made a speech once on the topic: 'Principal Teachings of Gandhism'. It had turned out to be a bad day for her as she forgot half of the speech and had ended it with '*Jai Hind*' abruptly, (we firmly believed that the Jai Hind completes the incomplete speech; a smart weapon to save ones face to certain degree). Teachers who loitered beside the dais expected her to open the damp sheet of paper that she clutched in her sweltered left hand, however she didn't. Though no one laughed publicly, there were concealed sniggers everywhere except me. I empathized with her feelings that day. It wasn't her mistake but of the crowd who diverted the flow of her by-hearted sentences with their unnecessary cheers.

It was my idiocy to suspect on Gopal of the authenticity in his accounts. I witnessed it clear in the day light. The man who proclaimed that 'the future of India lives in villages', now smiling bleakly and orphanly, not belonging to any of villages but hanging on the crossroads. I had no idea on what to do with the portrait. My mind suggested to take it off and carry it to the shrine. But what if they conclude that I too was a confederate in the Panchayat robbery? Let's not make it the story titled — 'Father stole it and the Son stashed it'. I brooded over the same, staring at the massive wooden framed portrait of Gandhi and his infantile smile. In the backdrop, at the unfocused area of the frame, Sumeru browsed, million miles away.

I heard the sound of a scooter flourishing gradually amidst the muffled roar of highway traffic and it seemed vaguely familiar. Before my mind could map it to the memory, it appeared on the road approaching me from the side of highway. It should be Doctor Revankar — Swathi's father. He must be returning from his work at Primary Health Centre, Kirsur. As the scooter came closer, my heart began thudding loudly for no reason and there was an unknown instinct that brought all my being into the presence at once. I was encountered by a wonder of wonders as the scooter passed by me and took a turn towards our village. It was Swathi who was sitting on pinion! With her long neck she turned back quickly and looked at me. That was the first time ever that I saw her dense thick hair streaming in the air, hitherto plastered with the *parachute* hair oil. She threw a reluctant smile at me, hiding behind her father's mighty build. The smile for which I used to wait at her door every evening. The smile for which I waited in many dreams. She appeared to have blossomed with an essence of poise, and an ethereal glow had sprung in her eyes. Like a pearl from the heaven of adolescence, a tiny red pimple on her right cheek shone along with her new nose ring. She, like forty kilograms of unadulterated magnet, pulled my heart and exerted a force on my impetus. A sudden thought tempted me to pursue her tout-de-suite. Before I could get onto my bearings, the scooter dwindled and receded at the slope near railway station and evanesced like a day dream.

I sit quiet amidst the rustle in the airplane-like library at the thirteenth floor and approach to ruminate on Mahatma, his notion and hypothesis of the villages. The soon I begin to think of villages, a sense of sheer pity and repugnance wells up in me, my heart strikes a riot — *They are the victims of so called globalization now. People of urban India appear to have committed intellectual suicide besides the people of the rural India committing the aesthetic and spiritual suicide. At the time when, Mahathma said 'The future of India lies in the villages' he wouldn't have anticipated anything of this technological revolution or repercussions of the last mile globalization. Now, they are neither the villages nor the towns, they are neither innocent nor matured, they turned to be a sort of hybrid settlements. A three storied construction of metropolitan facilities stands beside a shack that doesn't even possess a basic amenity like lavatory — testimonies of contradiction. A daily wage laborer, who struggles to earn three hundred rupees a day, uses a sophisticated device with internet facility, not out of conscious choice but out of imposed mass hypnosis by the corporates and social obligations. Youths of villages dream of becoming popular by any means, be it TV celebrities, film stars and internet sensations. This outlandish craving dominates their zeal for work and ingenious creation. Few of those who watch the clippings of millionaires and their ostentatious lifestyle, resort to open a liquor outlet at the edge of the village to suck out the money from the hardworking laborers and farmers. Buffaloes and the bullock carts disappear into the oblivion of time. Like the parthenium, a foreign weed that once brought from America, burgeoned everywhere rampantly, now the weed with the name of 'development' and 'modernity' mushrooming uncontrollably. Though it looks green, one shouldn't forget that it's after-all a weed.*

Those who owned agricultural lands have migrated to nearby towns and cities with the alibi of sophisticated education for their children and are fine with whatever the income that they gain from the farms.

Those who got furthered from the tides of change are settled in the cities and wash off their hands by sending fixed amounts of sums to their parents who dwell back in the villages. Consuming the western products has become a new lifestyle whereas the burden of self-identities like the race, caste, creed, lineage still rot and stink in the corners of their houses.

The disoriented individuals of the previous generation feel ashamed at times. Few try to adapt to the changes and create internet accounts wiping off the embarrassment on face and few lounge on the plastic chairs in the corners at homes, observing the lunacy of so called modern children with suppressed revulsion and swollen nerves. And the rest while away their time at temples and public places boasting of the glories of their bygone times.

I feel unsettled and tiptoe to washroom, avoiding the eye contact with the lipsticked solitary librarian who smiles at her device once in a while and seems engrossed all the time in amusing conversations, negotiating with her forelocks.

Oh, there he comes, in the mirror, the modern messiah, a progressive thinker, an aspiring social reformer, a future intellectual with a French beard and a lose pyjama, whom the media will generously label as a leftist. What do you cogitate all that for? Do you think you have any moral right to do that? You yourself are a victim, do you at-least realize it?

I get hammered by the resonating inner voice in that serene restroom.

I evade standing there too long looking into my own brown hazy eyes; urinate all of my thinking in shame and sidle back and settle on to my seat, beside the oval shaped window towards my left, and the coffee machine towards the right. There are rustles of newspapers and few whispers from between the book racks. In the distance she smiles again at the device with her glossy brown lips pulling her disturbing ringlets up, to place them behind the ear. *So what now?* I ask myself. The thinker in me subdues. Wispy strands of the cirrus clouds lose their identity as they float away through the oval frame.

I ambled back to Sumeru, after a sort of theatric experience offered by life. Let bygones be bygones. My heart had forgiven him already at subconscious level. We decided to ascend the hill before it gets dark. Sun was shy of time and still hovered behind. A peculiar thought sprouted in my mind while I made my way back guiding the horse. I began empathizing for Sumeru. *Why should he live here, hobbled, like a slave? I thought of his father and mother. They must have also labored all their lives under someone like Tonga Laal, groaning and grumbling, carrying immoral men on their shoulders.* At the same time, I thought of giving one more attempt to mount him. The scar at my elbow was a little dried with the warm wind and the bloody slit was caked with dust. At the curving of the hill, gave it a try by jumping partly and he dodged suddenly, pushing me away again.

Well, throughout the history, who gave man a sovereign persimmon to domesticate horses and use them as his servant carriers? Was there any consensus or the treaty signed between the chieftains of species of horses and humans? If the horses like man's company, it is all well and good, but who knows the heart of a horse? While the men fail to understand another human?

As I looked back from a view point, half way to the summit, there were tractors with trollies full of people rattled down the main road winding towards my village. Most of them wore colorful towels around their neck. I inferred someone should have died. Before could I establish myself, we encountered the lady with hijab. "Sharan Gowda is no more," she said placidly offering a handbag that contained few bananas and boiled sweet potatoes. She gazed at Sumeru in awe and suggested — "You should hurry, as it is getting late. Let us know if anything..."

It was dark by the time we reached Dargah.

Ajja didn't murmur anything that night. Rather, we heard a wolf howling and then began the faint music of *shehnais*. It was the song of the dead this time. As the silence began swelling, the howl intensified. I rose up and filled a glass of water and tiptoed to Ajja's room. He was fully awake with his eyes wide open, gawking at the infinite ceiling. I stood there at the door, peeping for a while as his eyes didn't blink. His hands on the chest, the guards of his bird shaked and thus I sneaked back to my bed, gulping the water, with deep sighs in the gaps. I grew numb for no reason though my scar experienced a cooling effect by the breeze, as coconut oil was applied for the same. Sumeru, at the left corner of the front yard, snorted once in a while.

Is he looking at the infinity? Is he imagining his afterlife? Is he preparing for his own death? He must be visualizing the ceremony at Sharan Gowda's. As the *shehnai* was accompanied by some *bhajan* songs, I was obliged to see it myself through the inner eye. *Sounds draw images when you keep your canvass ready.*

The stiff limbs of grand oldman must have been folded callously and they must have made him sit cross-legged on a table, against the wall with the support of a big X made by sticks under his neck and the clothes tethered to the pegs pulling his body. His swollen eyes must have shut and decorated with the thick glasses of him — with the right lens splintered.

In front of him should be old aged sisters and his daughters, keeping the vigil and manufacturing some hoarse cry, recalling and verbalizing the moments they spent with him. And then, outside the house, under the light of massive gas-lanterns, a herd of men, spread all over the blue tarpaulin mats, should be engrossed in discussing their own plight, perhaps about the seeds and fertilizers, and listening to the *bhajan* songs passively, dedicated to the life and times of the deceased.

Several men at the side deck of the house, on another tarpaulin mat, seated in a circle, playing cards, drinking and smoking, pretending to be discussing if the refreshments to the guests are arranged appropriately or not, though they have got nothing to do with the matter. And there, in the same circle, my father and Chennappa should be drinking from the leftovers from everyone's steel glasses.

"Hey sing loudly, he is the man who rode seven feet horse, he is the man who ruled this region like a king in older times, the greatest man ever lived in our village. It's the duty of all of us to send him off splendidly," my inebriated father should be ordering the vocalist of the *bhajan* troupe. Then the singer, who also flails and floats, begins a song of the local hero, of his adventures, replacing the original name in the song with the old man's. They all roar and applaud his sense of timing. The grand old-man celebrates the silence like he always did sitting on his *pyol*, watching over the passers-by with an eternal indifference through the pair of fractured lenses.

The silence emanated from Ajja's room was fierce than the noises. I sidled again towards his door. Those glittery eyes of him looked up like the candles but never flickered. In one, he held the life and in the other, the death.

Chapter 17

Trees also nap in the afternoons of the summit. In order to escape the choked desolation in the vacuum of the midday, I chose to wallow myself in the barn, feeding Sumeru. First the husk, and then the chaff, followed by an unknown affection. My fingers moved dexterously to wipe the rheum off the edge of his eye lids. A multihued dragonfly oscillating its diaphanous wings alighted on his back for a breathing space. Drongo, perching on its wonted place, sang a cryptic song like that of the Ajja's, wagging its long tail attuned to its song.

I was compelled to reassure myself that I am no more angry at him. It's the mistake of god that he fashioned the obstacles in communication along with his boastful varieties in the creation. Once in the past, Dhyami had rammed her foot on mine while in the excitement of hopping to her mother's udder. My last finger had become a piece of boiled carrot, but I was never mad at her. Sumeru must have regretted for his slip-up, he looked at me with the compassion of a buddha.

The dragonfly took its flight swiftly in the chunk of the moment to catch its next prey, or perhaps to find it's lost home.

That morning, while sweeping the floor with the homemade broom, an old torn-out piece of a paper, slid from under the door of the locked-up room and was bumped on to the bristles to coax me for one more attempt to demystify the enigmatic chamber. 'my legs are the pillars, the body the shrine, the head a cupola of gold', it read. I was compelled to read the lines twice or thrice, and that's it — they began to buzz like the bumble bees in the corner of my mind till the late afternoon. *Few moments of silence and few words of wisdom could get one inebriated in the wilderness.* I was placed on a swing of dilemma of whether to make another effort to unlock the door in the absence of Ajja or to leave it at that.

If my legs are the pillars and body the shrine, is my soul the god? If my soul is the god, I must also be the god then, for I am none other than the soul itself. If I am god, then where is the real god whom we all in quest of? In that case, every creature that possesses the soul qualifies to be a god. Are all the sinners and saints gods? Then, the world is full of supreme beings. If I put it in a different way, there could be one god and his essence be pervasive in every creature in the existence. Are we all like the tides on one eternal ocean underneath? Our life is nothing but the rise and fall of it?

Why go temples or mosques or churches then? Every mirror is a temple. Solitude is the prayer and silence the gospel. Inward journey is the greatest pilgrimage.

I ruminated like Sumeru did constantly, with his elongated jaws.

"darrrn... darrrn..." I heard a motorcycle emerging in the vicinity. Sumeru pricked his ears and dropped with a twinkle of curiosity in his blue eyes. I had come to believe that all the Drongos are born with sixth sense. Whenever it sang its song, visitors arrived without fail. The Suzuki motorbike took a decent roundabout and stationed in the frame of the doorway. They were two on the bike and I knew one among them.

"Lachya, get your satchel and come soon. Your father is very much ill," said the rider.

In response, I gazed at them with an impassive gait. When someone says, very much ill and you are asked to 'come soon'. It implied that something terrible has happened. I paced two steps further till the doorway and took a clear look at them again.

It looks to me that, they couldn't tolerate the awkward silence. I let few straws of hay to slip through the gaps between my fingers into the air, which I had held for no specific purpose.

"Your sister also has arrived from the city," the guy on the pillion got down from the bike while uttering it. I thought he would ask for some water to wash his mouth, or will walk till the bore-well under the tamarind tree, but he didn't care for either of them. He beckoned me while spitting his gutkha and gestured towards the bike to get on. The very moment, a thought thudded upon me like a missile from the sky and a huge cloud gloomed over — father should have been dead. My legs shuddered and the throat parched.

I made my way to the motorcycle and mounted, the other guy settled behind me — I was sandwiched in the thoughts as well. My lips hesitated to unpurse themselves even then. Motorbike started with a single kick and we embarked onto an uncanny journey. They turned out to be sweaty and miasmic. The pungent smell of gutkha that emerged from the rider's mouth made me dizzy. The sun hammered hard like never before. I essayed to frame my father in mind, about when I saw him for the last time. All I could recollect was his muffled speech, his slurred words that night while mother interrogated him; I had not got a chance to take a glimpse at his face then. He always seemed to be a mystery to me, for his deportment and the chaotic notions. At times, he sermoned like a remarkable moralist but his actions negated all that he spoke. There was never a chance that I got to sit with him face to face and talk of life looking right into his bloodshot eyes. He remained opaque all through his life. I had vexed at him when he tore off Ramanujan's portrait, as I had pasted it next to an old film star's.

Mother had told me once that father had won a big amount in *matka* on the day on which that actor's film was released. Howbeit, I was not against him or his apotropaic hero, all I despised was his intolerance, his immoral conduct, his addictions, his meaningless living, his distasteful being, his callousness, his everything except himself.

The ride was not as exhilarating as with the teacher Chaitanya's. All through the way, they did not speak either. The curves down the path of the hill made me even giddier. I dodged from the wafts of dust and the hot wind, and refuged behind the nape of the rider and began to brood on how to approach the scene where my father lies dead. There would certainly be the commotion of people gathered around, and the theatric acts of them who pretend to pity and console my wailing mother. Should I jump and dart into the gathering? Or sneak between the strangers and sidle slowly unnoticed and settle beside the body, like arrived from nowhere? I felt it would be a good idea to have a towel over my face, so that I could escape the people and their creepy eyes. Even if my emotions betray and I fail to manufacture the salty tears, the towel would surely save my bacon. I could hide myself under that; but where to find one? At the eleventh hour?

The rider took right turn from the railway station. I released my mouth to ask, "Why this way?" and was fed with an instant reply, "He is in Tarnal Hospital." For a moment, my jitters had come to a halt. The weight on the head was shifted onto the shoulder. I thought, the scene could be manageable in hospital. There would be two or three people around along with mother. It's always good to go to village with the mortal remains of father, like a real son, sitting beside him, combating flies and parasites.

After a mile or two, bike took the turn into a narrow mud-road that curved like a giant serpent between the endless corn fields.

"Short cut," the third man on the bike uttered before I even bothered to ask. I turned towards my right and the hill looked blue like before. The flag was swaying over our Dargah unchanged, still green. The humps and the bumps of the wild road loosened our joints beyond the doubts.

He pulled the bike over near a shed that was surrounded by a thicket of maize. It had a spacious clearing in the front, and a sizable verandah on which four men were busy playing cards sitting cross legged. A heat wave of deep confusion, swept through me shrinking my heart. The rider was none other than Pinto. He had not uttered a single word all through the journey. My naive propensity of thought attributed his silence to the seriousness at the matter of probable father's death. And also it had occurred to me that, in the small villages like mine, no matter how bitter they are, all the acrimonies and animosities tend to melt into collective empathy during the events like death and of that sorts. However, he was still the same — a snake in the grass. The man behind me clutched my arm as soon as I got down. Pinto went ahead and began washing his mouth with a cold gait, fetching water from a concrete cattle-trough, towards the right. A fat man with the bushy whiskers, who appeared standing in the frame of door at left end of the verandah that led to the mysterious interiors of the shed, beckoned us in the flash of light and disappeared into the room.

The guy, who held my arm, began to frogmarch me till the room. He loosened and tightened the grip in a peculiar rhythm based on his impulsive choices. I threw a look of demur at him when his clutch seemed would crush my tender bone. He appeared to have understood my concern and slackened it. Four men who were playing the cards turned their heads towards us in unison with the cunning and conspiratorial looks and ducked back to resume their game, as we moved past them.

The room had a tiny aperture that behaved shy to let the sun in. A heap of dry maize in the right corner and a pile of bamboo baskets in the other, couple of dry and crumbling ridge-gourd stacks were hung from the ceiling. The floor had an inexpensive red-oxide and was dusty all over. There stretched a charpoy along the right wall and an old wooden table with a chair placed in the middle. The shed had got all the merits to be called a farm-house had there been a lady around. There was a door at the end of the room that must have led to a store room.

"So Lachya, don't panic, your father is safe and sound. Nothing happened to him."

He stated sitting on the wooden chair, resting his elbows on the flailing table. His eye balls were boiled cherries. Though the words originated from mouth, eyes spoke more.

My arm was free as the guy had left me in-front of the conman and stood at the entry door watching us.

As I surmised, he turned out to be the man with the cleft-lip, whom, Gopal in his accounts, referred to as the conman of the region. His facial hair couldn't hide his broken lip.

"I heard you are offering the genuine numbers to the chaps from other villages whereas the wrong ones to our people, why is that so?"

I did not unlock my mouth. I had no idea of who were supposed to be our people.

He deliberately softened his voice so that I interpret it to be his sensibility to talk such confidential matters in whispers; to muffle it for the audience outside. But I knew, he still seemed to consider me to be an innocent and outcaste kid. Still, it was clear for me that all of these guys present around have planned it together — this conspiracy, this sordid stratagem to abduct me.

"Your father owes me some money," his voice croaked. I stood staring at his bemusing moustache and blood-red eyes. He cleared his throat and began to light a *beedi* striking the match on to the table surface.

"Don't take fright boy,"

He repeated, as it seems to me that, I might have let out some anxiety, like a helpless deer to be shot.

The first two strong puffs of him generated a small cloud of smoke between us. It made me even wobblier.

"You have reached a safe harbor well before his men would capture you. Sooner or later they will trace the leak, they will trace you, the men of Kantu Lal."

He spoke while drawing a triangle on the table with the dark head of a dead matchstick.

There was a commotion at verandah. Sounds of one man patting on other's back and then followed a shared guffaw. It must have been a game.

Light sunk drastically in the room. I seemed to have lost the sense of presence.

'He brings farm-labor girls to his shed and makes love. He lets his men to enjoy the free show from outside, through the gaps of the broken door.'

For a moment I turned back to take a glimpse at the entrance door, the guy was vanished and the door shut. It was solid with no holes or fissures. My eyes navigated towards the other door that led to an inner room. Yes. It was wretched. There were numerous vertical transparent stripes, few were filled with folded gutkha wrappers and the rest must have helped letting the eyes in. So, it didn't turn out to be a store room as I anticipated earlier.

"Don't worry. Let's settle everything. All we want from you is numbers. Open and Close for tomorrow and day after. So tell me soon and he will drop you wherever you wish to. Good for you, good for us, and for everyone."

He seemed to have got puzzled by my mental muddling and my strange fidgeting gazes towards both the doors. He must have thought that I was plotting for an escape.

'Nagul, is his name. He is the head gambler here; and he is the one, who bought your Kaali miscreantly.'

Gopal's words began to float around me, becoming one with the smoke. Instead of comprehending and digesting what Nagul said, my mind was still listening to Gopal.

"Why don't you speak? Have you lost your senses? I am asking you," he raised his voice a little, "tell me the number for tomorrow."

My helpless heart began a monologue within — I can't escape by passing a wrong number nor can I escape by revealing the genuine one, which I already have in my mind ready for the entire week. They will keep me in capture till the results are announced and till my prophesies are testified. They will bet all their wealth for the number that I share; if they win they get lot more money and will surely ask me for the next day's. If they lose all, they will surely kill me. They will get drunk for the night and will smack me till I die for 'playing the trick' with them. For a moment, there was a strong impulse that said — *they will kill and bury me in the midst of the corn field. There won't be a funeral. After few months, oxes will walk over my chest and the sharp edge of the plough will jab at my abdomen and disinter my corpse. 'Oh some boy, skeleton of a boy,' the stranger plowman will exclaim. He will lift the plough and proceed further, ignoring my corpse as it will be a sunset and too late for him to give a consideration.*

I fainted. The dim lit room turned ghostly dark.

*****

"Should we feed him something?"

"No, if he eats well, he will fall asleep. Let the hunger keep him awake, let it remind his obligation to us,"

"He will come out for sure, anytime, with the number, like a gentleman…"

"If he doesn't?"

"He will. We have time till the morning anyways. Let him figure out the right number for tomorrow."

"Are you chaps kidding? Let me get in and smack his head with these corn ears. Bastard will spit out whatever that he got in his shit head"

"Wait, not yet, not yet…"

I heard these voices, loud and clear. I knew they were all deliberate statements; to make me hear, to push me from all directions, a sort of bludgeon from outside.

When I woke up and got to my senses from the collapse, I found myself on the charpoy in his 'show-room'. There was an incandescent bulb that spilled the orange light, hovering over, to remind me of the passage of time. Its hanging wire was caked dark with gummy excreta of flies and their families. The tiny skylight in the middle allowed the evening breeze inside with its own terms and conditions. The striped door appeared locked up from outside. Few feet away, on the other side of the door, they gathered around the table and warned me indirectly. Even so, I maintained my pretense of the slept.

After a while, I overheard them leaving the room, perhaps towards the verandah, as there were sounds of motorbikes approaching. All I was confirmed with was a fact that, in either of the cases i.e whether I share them with the right numbers or the wrong ones, I would be killed.

'You may not believe, but the truth is — these were the men who murdered the Panchayat officer Mr.Betageri for merely ninety rupees! They got drunk, looted him roadside and threw his body away along with his moped into the giant quarry of Tarnal. They are not humans when they are drunk.'

Gopal's words fortified my extrapolations and inferences.

So, how about the roars of those motorcycles? They should be two or three in numbers certainly. They must have brought in parcels of drinks and fried chicken from the *dabha* nearby. It's undeniably the time to begin a never ending carouse.

"Come over soon, come over! Our fates will be changed in two days. We have found a goose that lays golden eggs…" I heard the muffled words followed by an uproarious guffaw.

Somewhere from nearby, through the thick darkness and the murmurs of drying maze, I heard the snorts. Was it Kaali?

Chapter 18

Between the endless shores of dusk and dawn, I drift and drown, born and die, meander towards the eternity. I immerse in the vigils and wait for the blue-light that could someday illumine my entire being. There are unremitting attempts to sync-up my pulse with the city's. Like the sea, the city has got its own voice; it reveals that enigma in the stillness of the night; I attune my hearing to that mystique symphony; beyond what I hear on the surface, it has its heart-beat obscured, like that of the hill. I keep my ears pricked up for it and wait for those whispers, which help me sail through this boundless sea. I grow rebel in the dreams and wake up to realize that I still swim with the tide. A heavy breath, an odd throb in the chest, a frightful nightmare reminds me of my mortal existence. I sit awake in the dead of the night and gaze at the infinity; behind the crystalline curtains a faint blue light from the far off land flickers and dies.

Those two pairs of eyes and a pair of dark disks, it's the third day in a row that I observe them espying on me. His inscrutable countenance complimented with those impenetrable sunglasses shield his persona thwarting all of my attempts to judge his motives. The other two, his accomplices seem to be born-confederates. They fit in nowhere but in the midst of random crowd who cunningly espy on the target from over the shoulders of their ringleader, drawing the clouds of cigarette smoke that affects the view at them. As soon as I descend from the sky-train station, step by step in the dying light of orange sun, they follow me, those eyes, till I walk further and drift into the ethnic crowd of Market Street. I don't turn back, but make my way faster and sidle into the obscure residential alleys dodging the uncertainties, where children struggle to take the turn with their bicycles and stray dogs pop up like automatic bollards. Nevertheless, all of them steer clear their way from me, or vice versa. At last, I grope through the stairs and make it to the room. Before changing, I stand overlooking the front street through the gaps of curtains parting them nimbly, in case if they followed me all along.

I question my vigor that says, 'Talk to her, talk to them and settle the matter.' After a minute or two an answer subdues the question — 'There's nothing to be talked or settled off.' I roll the matter up and push it into the attic of my mind and it unrolls back even wider and longer posing a grave challenge. I keep aside the food parcel that I brought and vent to cook on my own, to engage myself into a different art; to make sense of my sterile existence. I tend to like chopping the onion for no reason. It is the only thing on earth that could well up tears in me. I cope-up with it only till its lachrymatory agent invades the very core of my perception. I drop the idea and the halves of onions into an empty vessel and wash off the hands at it.

In the fullness of time, I attempt to tame my mind and oblige myself to sit down to conjure-up a few lines on the page. None of the words volunteer to come to the fore. They behave intransigent like a teen girl in whom the sense of rebellion dawning. *Vine in a hanging pot, grows downwards, thinking it's roots are underground* — I write such lines after knuckling down myself, and erase them off in ignominy. Within a matter of few blinks of the eye, I drift into a numb trance. An unheard of gravity pulls me deeper and deeper. The senses go inward like that of the limbs of a tortoise. My eyes forget to blink and I get stupefied. *Why did it all happen?* Asks my inner voice as I struggle to overcome the matter that seems to be aggravating exponentially with the time — the misery of being chased by unknowns and myself.

The spells of self-pity are more gratifying than the wildest of the masturbations. I reflect. Most of the human population has multifariously self-victimized in many aspects. The victims of colonialism, victims of class oppression, victims of racism, victims of what not. Thus I refuge into one. I am a victim, not just me, all of us.

That vast sports ground, with the fine red soil hanging in the air, reflected the fierce sun so emphatically that the entire atmosphere was toned with lurid orangish hue. I had pressed myself with the empty belly on to the fence with my tender fingers entwined into the mesh of it. Yes I was tender, like a young vine. The voice in the loudspeaker reverberated through the entire area and the lethargic pulses of crowd ascended to the unheard of heights at once. Stage was too far and was obscured behind the illimitable lines of populace; thus it was hard for me to figure out the source of that enchanting base voice. All I could witness was the people seething and muddling at the fringes, few meters away from the fence where I waited.

'You will all be victims, each one of you, and your children too. We should all get onto the roads and the streets and protest to save the smell of our soil, to save our colors, to save our tongue, to save our garb, to save our tastes, to save our milieu, to save our indigenousness, to save ourselves. If not now, then never. We don't need this venomous octopus called globalization at our houses. It's a conspiracy of some vested interests to cripple our organic growth, to slit the throat of our culture. Don't agree and offer your consent for the development of fertile lands into commercial sites around the fringes of our city. Once the transnational companies steady their roots here, there will be an incommodious influx of migrants for jobs. So there will be demands for temporary residences, apartments, paying guest hostels and so on; and then the land rates will soar, house rents will be augmented exponentially. Nonetheless, no matter how long they stay here, all those migrants, they will never feel our town as their home, our taste as theirs, our interests as theirs, all they do will purely be business, strictly the commerce devoid of ethics, all for money.

Then will you witness the mushrooming of alien restaurants, sky scrapers and western-like apartments and also, in their shadows, small complexes devoid of aesthetics, with the sole mercantile interests. Two decades down the line, you won't afford a square-foot of land in your own town. None of us will. Hence the people will begin to find shortcuts and that in a seriatim, triggers the rampant corruption, illegal trade and the flow of black money and so on. It will all end in an incorrigible disorder, in a sheer chaos. Come with us, we will forestall all this nonsense; we will nip it in the bud; we will ram the head of this venomous octopus. Else you will all be victims of it, all of you…"

The blaring words of the speaker echoed from all the directions to create a tumult among the disoriented crowd; rather, I waited for the speech to conclude. A middle aged fellow audience had enlightened me with his suggestion already — "The food after the speech." I rushed to join the queue behind him like a rightful consumer. The crowd could cause a deadly stampede if was not handled appropriately. I got my comfortable share — the hot *pulav* (vegetable rice) and a glass of buttermilk. That was more than what my long starved belly wished for. We walked towards the gallery to sit down and munch it peacefully, relishing the spectacle, the fight for food, the fight for the rights. "Such a pessimistic view; if your culture and ethos are so strong, they will survive no matter what; why feel so insecure and sinister? It's an act of wickedness to protest the development. As long as you don't have your own model of development, you have to borrow from others. India should develop in first place, and then it's apparent that the people will fight for their ethnicity and will protect it, if they wish to. You don't realize the efficacy of your home food, until you taste all sorts of continental and foreign recipes. It's pure ignorance and selfishness on his part," the anonymous guide of mine, murmured while gobbling all that he fought for. I couldn't get what to respond with, hence smiled and nodded at his views. What placed me in a little surprise was, unlike the people of my region, here in this city, they at-least spoke of event rather than merely grumbling about the free food served.

Humanity is divided by the dietary traditions but is united by the hunger. With the time, with the food, there grew an affectionate amicability between us. Soon after polishing off the plates, he asked me of my whereabouts and my plans. I tried my best to be true.

He walked me till a public library, under the shade of lush green avenues. As we stood in-front of an old gate with a fine-looking filigree, he looked thoughtful and picked up a pebble from the roadside and tied it in a white cloth that he fished from his pocket.

"What is it that you said your name was?" he asked scratching his black and white beard.

"Laxman Chalavadi sir."

He adjusted his thick glasses and looked pensive again.

"Hmm, so let's make it Laxmish C then,"

He said surveying at the red petals of Gulmohar which were scattered all along the pathway that ended at the porch steps of the library.

I found it to be amusing — the process of changing my name.

"You can go to a temple and smear the holy ash on your forehead, and wear this around your neck," he garlanded me with the cloth pendant in which the oval shaped pebble was wrapped and locketed.

"Now you look like a real soldier of shiva, a *veerashaiva* with a *saaligrama,*" he pinched my cheek with his long robotic fingers.

"You see that building over there?" he pointed towards a timeworn edifice that looked like a boarding house, "just go there and request them that you want to get admission and then you leave the rest for god to take care."

"Thank you Sir" I thanked him cursorily, as I was unsure of whether I will go knock the door of that refuge or not.

"Don't slip your tongue to tell them your old name in a hurry." He patted on my back and retreated into that splendid architecture with a huge board that read, State Central Library.

I was obliged to follow the advices of the nobleman as I had no other option. The pebble that hanged in my neck was a little heavy; but it surely had a purpose, a purpose of identity and a purpose of life in itself.

I prowled about the streets for a temple, where they keep the round block of holy ash *vibhuthi* at their disposal. Eventually, I came across a roadside temple that seemed to enjoy the patronage of locals; however, it was deserted for an unknown reason, may be for it was late afternoon — the time when even the god slumbers. There were no one around, save for the lord shiva himself, lounging in silence in his abode. I washed my face and smeared three horizontal chalk-white stripes on my forehead, as bright as Swathi's. I must have surely looked like the modern disciple of philosopher Basava of twelfth century. Had I gone in this avatar to any of the houses in my village, I would surely have gotten enough offerings in alms — rotis, flour, coins, cereals and what not.

I paced up and down around the temple to manufacture a sort of courage; the courage to carry out an adventure, the audacity to take a leap of faith. I looked myself in a broken mirror placed under a long-standing sacred fig. I couldn't believe it was me. My external look had gone through a sort of metamorphosis. Having walked half of the city barefooted for last two days and having slept in the railway station, my skin was tanned like never before. Sun is indisputably the same everywhere — unsparing. Three white bars against my dark brown forehead looked contrast and perfectly salient on my face. In order to make it look a little natural, I wiped the edges and bedimmed it's radiance with the hem of my shirt. Even then, there was an indomitable dilemma — *should I go there? Or is it better to go back to the bus stand? Or is it judicious to keep exploring a little more?* I arrived at a conclusion before long and began a measured pacing towards the antiquated house. When the left hesitated, the right was resolute and when the right grew reluctant, the left remained undaunted. *The clerk at the office wouldn't send me to jail for my trivial and tailored lies,* is what I had put a seal on in my mind. The pathway from the gate was all speckled with the copper-pods and gulmohars. It looked like a yellow-red carpet for the new guest laid by the god himself.

The idea of my temporary guru had worked out a great deal to some extent. The clerk at the reception was impressed with my avatar, confidence and the lies toned with perfection. However, there still was a stumbling block. Provoked by my flawless facade, he was compelled to ask a question that sounded a little out of syllabus for me at this impromptu encounter.

"Can you tell me any of the Vachanas of Basavanna if you happen to know?" I stopped filling the form as he had suddenly put me off my stroke. I stood agape at the register and his surveying eyes, below the pinched forehead furrows. "This is how you get caught," said a ghostly voice in me. A small bust of Basavanna on the table, perhaps carved out of a hard sandstone, seemed to be laughing at me.

"Don't you know any?" he pressed again.

"The rich will make the temples for shiva; what shall I, a poor man do? My legs are the pillars, the body the shrine, the head a cupola of gold…listen, o lord of the meeting rivers, the things standing shall fall, but the moving ever shall stay…" I uttered closing my eyes in one go.

"Very good, this is what I expected," he patted on my back, a little harder.

I have no idea, how those lines were conjured up and manifested voluntarily and also how deep they were engraved on the leaflets of my memory; those same lines that were slipped out from the secret sanctuary of Ajja.

From the window of my new room in third floor, I contemplated at the maroon-colored architecture — State Central Library — obscured behind the lines of gulmohars and copper-pods, greened here and there by the tapestry-like mosses; past that was the ground where I met my life changer and bore the roaring speech of an unknown conservationist.

It is strange yet natural that my mind gnawed his speech only after quenching my thirst and satiating the hunger.

For the next few days, those pressed words of him — 'victims', troubled me a little. *What is it to be a victim? I thought. When he said 'all of you will be victims', was I also included in that? Did I land into a land of future victims?* There was a constant churning at my subconscious that went on for years. During the classes and prayers, my ears were hammered by the fierce words swollen by the megaphones and massive aluminium loudspeakers. The words that stood pro and against the dystopian octopus called globalization. Every so often, there were outbursts of harangues by the politicians — the words were so blaring that the spiders in my room climbing the walls used to get dropped on to the floor by their sound and start again when the speeches were done.

Now, at this hour of night, I attribute all of my difficulties and conditions to the same venomous octopus that he ranted of. If I wasn't put up in an apartment like this, I wouldn't have met her; I wouldn't have maintained a regular intimacy with much ease like this. The idea of building a luxury apartment of this sort is evidently the brain child of that octopus. And it is the culprit of all the sins. Yes, I am the victim, the victim of this nocuous octopus sting. I convince myself and struggle hard to shut my eyes.

My hand goes to pick up the transparent coffee cup. The ice has already melted, and I sip it. My tongue goes neutral about the taste. The cup is brought home from my favorite coffee shop, which is factually built on the grave of my childhood hostel. There are no copper-pods now, no gulmohars, no spiders, no children and nothing, but all the strangers, opaque people who smile through the transparent walls.

After my exit from the hostel, for higher education, the trust had sold the building for a multinational coffee shop chain and was shifted to outskirts. I doubt if any student goes there now. I visit that coffee shop frequently to find myself. My post flee memories are buried there along with time. A receptionist who speaks in forced accent sits at the place where I sat and studied all the night in a dim light for my exams. A line of cars are parked where I took my ablutions. Artificial trees and fountains spring where the gulmohars blossomed. I gape out from the glass wall of second floor. There, I witness the shabby central library, struggling hard to save itself. Beyond that, the ground, a little contracted, hosts evening walkers. About few yards yonder is the railway station, behind which, the rail tracks are stretched infinitely, and towards their end is my childhood where the sky leaned forward to embrace the earth.

Chapter 19

I find myself amidst the endless debris of shattered buildings. There's not a single structure left erect in the city. In better terms, there is no city left. All the roads are strewn with the broken computers, cables, silicon boards and all sorts of electronic waste. Sky trains hang from the elevated corridors like the snakes from the treeless branches. There are no humans to be seen around. I attempt to gauze as far as I could, there are no one. Here and there, the smokes rise up from the heaps of microchips creating the toxic clouds.

I am in the driver's seat of a yellow-colored bulldozer with the label — Laxman Earth Movers — written in black over its boom. What am I there for? Maybe to clear off all the wreckage; or perhaps I was assigned the task of demolishing all the skyscrapers, apartments and everything around — the task of the annihilator, a form of Shiva; or possibly I am entrusted to plan it new, to reconstruct everything afresh — the task of the creator — The Brahma; or is it that I am cursed to sit there and witness helplessly? The fall of everything? The way I beheld its rise? Helplessly?

I wake up before I could figure out the meaning of such bizarre dream.

All that one craves for, in a locked up room is an air of freedom. Every breath gets warmer and conscious in the boiling furnace of time. The beads of the sweat that glide and fall down possess the gravity of one hundred oceans. The wrinkled canvas of the mind gets filled up with the colorful imaginations of macabre nature. A ghost of the self, manifests on the wall to convince one — this is what you are born for: to suffer forever, and to transform that suffrage to the very nature of your being; to struggle forever and to transform that struggle to the very purpose of your existence.

A heap of onions in the corner, sprout in the dark silence — a form of agitation? Or an effort to prove their independence from the soil? Few among them must have rotten; their sleek that spreads throughout the room seems to imply that the captivity smells pungent.

There lingers another faint smell in the background; it must be of the droppings of a horse; not like that of Sumeru but of the wooden horse standing on the side-table of my bed — stale and stink. In the inky corners of the wardrobe, my old perfume resurrects intermittently and teases the new one.

A cracked egg of a sparrow on the floor waits for the fruit flies — a life, a dream lay broken for the sustenance of many lives. All that one could offer to this existence is oneself, says the unborn soul of the sparrow.

Wheezes of the chilling winds, dog-barks in the distance, few snores and the fading sound of the metro train proclaim that the night isn't the same everywhere. A dilemma of whether to contemplate on rewinding the time to yesterday or to leap into a tomorrow of the unknown, loiters in a corner like an unsatisfied phantom.

The loneliness echoes the chaos.

When the door is locked from outside, one tends to feel stifled and fights to break free. If it is locked by oneself from inside, he remains alright. In both the cases the door is locked and the man is in incarceration. *Many are self-locked and the rest are locked up by others* — I reflect being myself. The bulb that hangs over me, knows well of what it takes to live in the detention and the isolation. Though it has got all the powers to glow like a mini sun, it surrenders at the feet of the darkness unless coaxed by an energy. They speak of smashing my head, slitting my throat, breaking my limbs and many vile desires to subject my body into. The mesh of charpoy, those strands of rope already induce a feeling of the captivity, of a wild beast wriggling in a net as they lift it to transport. That suffocation, the sense of unfreedom pervades into the very bones of my existence. Yet, there is a wild thought that doesn't shy off to poke me — this is where he made love to numerous women. Their moans and sighs must have intertwined with the jute mesh. They smell of sweat unquestionably, they make pressed marks on my cheeks. There's a deep ache at my right bottom and I sense that the pain is fresh. They must have kicked and failed to wake me up, when I fainted.

I hear the treads in the passageway. Is it a man or a woman? Is it one or three? I strain my ears to make out. There's a hammering roar of the motorcycle starting, which sends its sound ripples to plague the feeble sleep of humming birds and the insects. They must have run out of the liquor or the meat. I hear the crattle of many feet at once scurrying towards the door. I pretend to throw myself into a realistic sleeping posture. The door opens; they must have seen my eyes closed with my chin pressed against the netting of charpoy. He knocks at the already opened door — one-two, four-five in a rhythm. I cower and pretend to be deep asleep. He locks the door up and leaves. An inexplicable tremble, a wave of deep angst rattles my being constantly. He would come in and beaten me up, if he was inebriated till the brink of his neck and the senses. He gives it a consideration for another round of drink, for a little more concession in time for the ceremony.

The image of Laila flashes in-front of my eyes like the lightning — her body, the way police men carried her corpse out of her house, wrapped up in the swinging blanket, chased by several houseflies. I and Nilesh had witnessed the scene from his terrace. Laila lived few houses away from mine. She was younger than Rani by a year or so, however, was still her classmate — a victim of a general notion in our locale — the earlier you send them to school, the sooner they grow up. In-fact she was the victim of many other things. Laila was yet another cursed flower in the bouquet after Shaila. Laila — Shaila — they rhymed in the fate too.

In the words of a newsman — on a fateful day, her mother had been to work consigning one hundred rupees to the tender hands of Laila for some unknown purposes. Her inebriated father, being aware of her possession, nagged her for money in the sleepy afternoon. After facing several denials, he smacked her at last and her head was rammed into the sharp edge of an wooden pole and that's it. There was a shiny bead of blood in her left ear dripping down and she sank into the oblivion. He managed to truss her neck to the pole with her own *dupatta* and cried his throat out to gather the people. He was spared from the judicial punishment, as the people around aided him to prove it a suicide. However, the ill-fated man began to drink even more, day in and day out and rolled over the street crying, bellowing, groaning and grovelling like an age-old stray canine for the next few nights; and at last disappeared from the village; no clue of his existence thereafter.

There is a wooden pole in here too, in this very room, waiting for a young skull. For the next few minutes or so, there are no sounds except the whispers of corn crops around. The motorcycle arrives bringing in the deep roars piercing through the dark night.

There are sounds of soft voices conversing in excitement in the front-yard. They begin their second spell of drinking in no time.

There are constant knocks at the door; I sit awake, "Who the hell is it?" I want to scream. I hold back. Silence befalls again like the mood of a young widow. I stare at the door with eyes wide open. They don't seem to be there — no shadows, no whispers, no sounds of breathe, no presence at all. My hunger keeps me wakeful.

The flame in me begins to die, I seem to give in and slip into a deceptive dizziness. Even the lamb that was brought from Bijapur for the sacrifice in Dyamavva's fair, resisted and fought for its life till the grumpy man with giant whiskers hammered with a honed axe on to its scruff. *Am I too puny to live? Is this what I left my home for? To die a death of an unknown?* The soul of that lamb must now be laughing at my cowardice; there spring the echoes of it everywhere.

I fiddle and probe, like a caged wolf on its first day in the confinement, which paces up and down drawing a pattern of 8 on the ground. The hope sustains the effort and the effort sustains the hope. On the spur of the moment, I find myself struggling to move a half gunny bag of maize, away from a tarpaulin curtain and succeed. It's the concealed backdoor! I push open it hard, and it doesn't move. There seems to be a weight placed against the door outside. I mount up all of my energy to give one more attempt. Nerves at my neck and the temples swell and my stomach almost crushes till it touches the spine. I push it with my right shoulder, like a raging bull, like a Sisyphus pushing the boulder up the hill. After a mighty force, there's a deep sound of thunder — a huge cauldron, full of water thuds on to a hard rock and rolls over. I fall out hurting my arm and rise up to stumble onto a stack of thorny firewood. Few tiny springs of blood originate in my palms, right-leg and where else? I compose myself and disappear into the dark matter between the never ending corn crops. Gushes of blood at the sole get blocked by the fine and cold mud. I run and pant and run like an old dog suffering a grave attack. I scamper in an unknown direction. 'You will be hunted soon, you will be chased in no time' — screams my heart.

I hear them maneuver in the distance but there's no clue of light to be seen. After reaching the first dyke, I make out the gleam from the shed and discern the motorcycle starting. I assure myself that there is no option but to grope through the tenebrous corn fields. As I go deeper it grows taller. I maintain my direction away from the sound of motorcycle and the main road. Mother had once told me of the foxes in the thickets of corn crops. My leaps grow wary with the image of foxes in mind. The blood drops freeze in the chilling weather but the pain transforms into a despair and agony. Every long leap that I jump, takes me closer to the freedom — says my heart again, even in that misery. As I reach another boundary-dyke, the watery fine mud of the deccan at the mouth of embankment squelches between the fingers cooling my sores. I ignore the provocation of my mind to lie down and sprawl up. Sky looks all blue, and the stars seem to be enjoying the show, smiling at my providence. I pant hard, the sores in the sole suck up the soil and burn even more.

It must be few minutes to the breaking of dawn, the time for ghosts to retreat to their graves. I see the wings grown on the shoulders of the wooden horse perched on my side-table; a gleam of silvery light emanates from its eyes. It seems to have got into life.

There appears to be a roar of motorcycle and the yellow beam coming towards me from the left, thus I take a deep turn towards my right. *There is no better compass than the moon and the stars for the one who is breaking free.* I reach the same boundary-dyke with the wet mouth and mount up on it.

As I turn back to survey, there are gleams of three torches swaying and engaged in the hunt for me, not too far. I seem to give in; tears well up in me. An unknown thirst makes me faint, and I haul myself forward as quickly as I could. I can hear them clear now, they are somewhere in the closer proximity hiding the torches. There are murmurs of corn crops being disturbed by them, and the gasps that sync up with mine. I run along the dyke to move away from their pace.

Images of me, dying by their empty bottles cracking my skull and my burial in the same field flashes over the horizon. I feel to be losing the breath, may faint anytime. At the end of the hedge, I plummet into a gorge. *Should I scream out loud? 'Sixty three is your number, please don't come after me'.* I want to shout but I don't. I rise up suppressing all the pain and begin darting along the boundary-dyke again catching the breath.

The deep buried giant wakes up within me. I bolster myself to face it. 'If not now, then never' — I coax myself to take the plunge. The broken chord of the violin needs to be fixed; the left out page in the diary needs to be filled up; the path that was ignored needs to be walked; the incomplete poem needs to completed; the garden of the forgotten dream has to be visited. The rainbows are to be drawn again. The wooden horse begins to flip its wings; it levitates, floats and flies away breaking the window to soar higher and higher till it reaches the splendorous sun, slowing down the time that it hefted. I rise up, open the door, and descend the stairs. There seems no one on my way to ask where am I heading to. I wake my long dormant car up and drive away dispelling the darkness. I steer through the avenue of streaks of light as though crossing the galaxies in the unbound cosmos.

There seem to be a narrow road in the distance. All of my pains keep me awake and alive. As I reach the end of the dyke i.e. the end of the corn field, I descend and take a long hop to escape the gorge. My acumen goes blank all at once. I perceive the presence of warmth in the vicinity, of an unrecognized affection and an intimate saga. I meet up with a mystifying vision. It's Sumeru, he stands there, waiting for me, like my destiny. I mount with no second thought but he doesn't stir. In a moment or two, he begins to gallop. A heavenly joy falls upon me dominating all the woes and miseries. It's the dawn. The breeze takes me alight like a quill, I feel out of the body. I turn back and it's all dark. In the distance towards my left, there is a glimmer of light. Sumeru knows the route, I think. All I do is to hold him tight as he jumps small hedges through the narrow road.

The glimmer turns out to be the railway station. There are one or two waiting for the train, signal says the train is about to arrive. The same motorcycle waits there at the parking. As we moved closer, I could make out that it is Pinto, at the entrance near the ticket counter, smoking a *beedi*, and waiting for me. The train shrieks and arrives. Sumeru moves further, sneaking past the entrance, till the end of the fence, near the park and stiffs its limbs. The last bogey of the train is merely meters away. I get down and wait, the train shrills again to depart. Sumeru whinnies, I dart across the platform and jump into the train as it moves. Sumeru looks at me from far as I hide behind the door and gape through the glass. He moves away and dissolves into the slope towards the hill. Pinto, under the shimmering light smokes his last puff and watches on the departure of the train. The heart beat and the train sounds blend themselves. It chugs along faster. Through the window, in the distance I witness the water-tank and the godown in my village. They too move away like toys and dissolve into the oblivion. The chilling wind and the warm berths, snores of the passenger on the opposite bunk, gather up a nap within me.

*****

The golden rays of the sun make my eyes squint. 'Is this what you wanted?' Asks the bird in my breast. I utter 'yes' in a delirium. It sings the song of the glory of the morning sun along with the chorus of all the sparrows around. For the first time in life, sun goes gentle on me. I walk into the never ending green plains; the ecstasy of drinking up the oceans, moving the mountains, flying above the clouds spring in me at once. The beads of dew rejuvenate my person. There's a light passing through the spine glows up my eyes, the blue light that I waited for, in my long vigils. I become a butterfly that is charmed by a long hedge of mirabilis — pink, yellow and multihued, and the jasmines from the paradise. The birds in the sky create patterns as I sprawl — as though they sign on the empty page of my heart. I grow intoxicated with the fragrance, with the love, with the compassion in the laps of mother-nature. The tears of joy condense into the pearls and shine along with the dew drops.

Chapter 20

Skies are pink; nestlings dance fervently on their toes to enfold their exhausted mothers on their arrival; crickets prepare to their concert for the eventide; in the distance of few paces, silhouettes of palm trees hover like the specters of our ancestors, benumbed by the jolt of time. The pond invokes a sort of twilight coldness and a kind of cologne that can wet any random mind. My meditation on the lotus, on its birth, on its beauty, on its evolution, on its death and on its decay is disturbed by a call, "It's late, please come for coffee." I stir up to escape from the apotheotic annihilation with the lotus. It's the second time from the bench in the gazebo beside the pond from where I address, "I will be there in a while."

Every so often, Mothi my exotic German shepherd vigils with me; pricking his ears, raising his eyebrows now and then, waits for a miracle to happen. He appears to think that I wait for a dolphin or of that sort to rise up all of a sudden from the serine pond; or that I am on a prowl to hunt a rare aquatic creature. Someday, he will know that the silence itself is the miracle that I yearn for, the utter stillness.

Lights are turned on in the house and it's time to walk back.

I while away my mornings and evenings contemplating on the pond, strolling through the green alley in the palm-grove listening to the chirping birds, relishing the glory of the buddings of flowers and the blushing vines that serpent to the fence-poles and soaking my feet in a small silvery stream that flows across through the farm. Every now and then, I sow the seeds of varieties of mangoes, along the water channel and witness them sprouting up — the chaste, heavenly wine-colored saplings, that reveal the lineaments of the creator. Like a man molded out of mud, I crave for the intimacy with the earth.

On a serendipitous morning, I discover a pendular-nest fallen on the scrubby ground beside the well. I take a mindful perusal of it to find out that there are no eggs, nor the mother present in its chamber. 'It must be Baya Weaver', I assume. I pick it up to carry back home, appreciating its elaborate and meticulous fibrous craft, hanging it in my hand the way it did in tree before it's tumble. At the halfway, I seem to halt by a sharp awakening — *what do I do with it at home?* All I could do is to hang it on the wall to the peg above my study table — what for? Perhaps for a fortuitous inspiration, to produce two or three lines of prose. Is that all? Robbing someone's life for poetry? I take a roundabout and walk back towards the well. I am aware of poets who attend the funeral of strangers only to produce few lines. *I don't fall into their category* – my heart convinces itself. I secure the nest as tightly and as naturally I could, to the branch of Indian Jujube that leans over the well. *What is the guarantee that the bird will occupy it again?* A question pushes me again into a conundrum as I trudge back to home. From that day forward, I journey and visit the nest to check if the lost guests are arrived — and make it a part of my daily morning routine. So far, it hangs empty. *What if the bird stalks at me and is aware of my visit every day? Is that the reason it doesn't want to come back? Did the bird sense my smell in the nest and discarded it forever?* Many such wild questions mushroom together. I know how laborious is it to construct a house having experienced myself. I want to spare that entire effort for it, if not the same bird, any other is also welcome to occupy it. I decide to cease to visit the nest for few days — but with a hope of their arrival.

*****

Father is long gone. Mother is here with me in the farm-house. We have a water buffalo and a cow — though not named them yet. I have married an appealing country bred girl, an orphan, chosen by my mother. When mother says, "She was an orphan", I reply, "We are all orphans in some way or the other." She throws a dismissive look that says, 'You seem to have lost your senses.' Ruthu is her name. It means seasons, in native language, however she remains same whole through the year. All that she knows is to cook, to work in the farm in her free time and to celebrate the silence, wearing an interminable smile, better than any other flower around. "We need not hurry for kids for at least one or two years," I say in the midnight caressing her belly as soft and warm as the fertile red soil of our farm. Like the earth, she doesn't reply anything, except a submissive nod that says 'as you say'. "Why are you afraid of kids?" Perhaps she wants to ask, but she doesn't. I too have no idea of the answer. Nonetheless, she loves children. I discern it by her affectionate conduct towards Rani's children during their visits. There's a conjuncture forming in my mind that on a night filled with the burning libido, she might strike a mischief by hiding or throwing away the contraceptive, to subject me for a test. It wouldn't bother me much, I suppose.

Whenever it rains, in the midst of my gazebo session, she seems to think that I badly want to get back to the home. Thus, she hurries up till me with an umbrella, flailing and lifting her strawberry-patterned saree up till the knees, painting her saree-bottom with the mud by her slippers. Under the gazebo, she stands blank and looks at me muddling with the umbrella. I expect her to speak, she doesn't. "Why are you on the move always, running here and there like a squirrel? Come sit here," I order her in a serious tone offering a seat beside me on the bench. Mothi looks at us perplexed wagging its tail. She follows my gaze towards the pond quietly. There are numerous ripples in the pond created by every drop, one wave pushing the other aside. I attempt to envisage the frame of her mind at the moment; she turns back towards the left to confirm if mother catches the glance at us by any chance. The rain intensifies and few thick drops invade our space. "What are you thinking about?" I ask her without changing my regard. "Nothing," she replies. "What are you looking at?" "Nothing." these are the most celebrated answers every day. 'Nothing' — for everything. I rise up and she follows. Mothi overtakes both of us and sprints on the boundary-dyke, chased by the fierce rain drops.

Little annoyed by her sense of over solicitude tinted with the blatant servitude, I lecture her in the middle of the night — "You are not my slave; neither my attendant. You should enjoy your own space and should possess your own likes and dislikes. You have got all the freedom here. You have the equal rights and privileges as much as I do on everything about us here. Do you get it?" I ask her looking right into her blue eyes like a boss. She smiles and ducks her head proceeding to slide under the blanket placing her cheek over my hairy chest, perchance to enjoy the chaotic heartbeats. *Does she understand? Or she pretends to be ignorant?* I don't seem to unravel. I turn off the lights and overlook through the window, towards the entrance, one of the gate-light flickers but Mothi doesn't bark. The faint murmur of the silvery stream reaches my ears like the whispers of god. *It needs to be fixed;* I utter within myself and doze off.

We have two rooms upstairs — our bedroom and my study. There's a personalized library in my sanctum. I work there from morning to evening — mostly on number theory and the literature towards the end, like the pudding. Though the sums no more appear like the rainbows, I work on many theories that could somewhere help the mankind in future in the field of artificial intelligence and in the study of motion of fluid in space and so on. *Are you behaving superficially ambitious?* I ask myself on a quiet afternoon. The sticky notes at my desk reads, 'short term goal — to solve the Riemann Hypothesis'. How long is the short-term? It seems unmeasured and unfathomed. If I turn my head towards the right over my shoulder I can see the entire farm till it's end, through the massive triangular window — the pond, coco-grove, flower hedges, vegetable plots, the stream, and the endless sky. It is from here, that I catch her glimpses surreptitiously most of the times, while she gets herself busy with scything the weed through the lush green coriander and spinach plots. I certainly get caught and turn myself red, then pretend to watch past her towards the coco-grove thoughtfully, resting my chin on palm with the forefinger on cheekbone. 'How childish of you?' she must have teased behind that smile.

There rests a black and white portrait of MK Gandhi on the left wall, right above the rack of volumes — there seem to be no more moral-liability or the remorse persists now which could prevent me to look at him with the free mind.

If there are knocks at the door, it's always her, reminding me of my duty to feed myself and Mothi.

I gaze at the lotuses and their shadows, those subtle petals — partially opened enigmatic wombs where the sun slumbers. When I contemplate at them in the morning, my heart comes to a full bloom. I become one with the tranquility. I feel obliged to recollect the underlined words from one of the essays that we wrote in school about the lotus — beauty, purity, majesty, grace and serenity. I ponder upon each of them. *The faith in the light, the vigor to plunge out from the mud and the sustained nobility to remain unstained by the past is what makes it a lotus,* I reflect. In the secret most corner of my mind, I conspire to live like a lotus, as a lotus, buoyant, in full bloom, untainted. I even give a thought of writing a one line biography of them — 'Beauty is in the flower, not at its roots'.

No matter how hard I try to be in the here and now, once in a while, I tend to grow retrospective. That evening, when my wife wallowed herself in plucking the vegetables and flowers for the night, I decide to broach the topic of my curiosity. Streaks of evening sun that penetrate the massive windows of the hallway, color my mother's profile with the lurid orange hue. "How did he die, father? Were you there beside when he was breathing his last?" I ask her in a curious voice. Mother's hand, that was busy picking out the grains of sand meticulously from a tray of broken rice, halts for a while as she replies — "He is not your father, you were already born when I married him." There strikes a sudden clang, of a metal container being kicked off by someone outside. "Then who is my father?" I want to ask but I don't, surmising an instant reply — "How does it matter now?"; mother, places the tray nimbly on teapoy, clasps the polished hands of oak-chair and rises up with a sigh, saying, "It's time for milking, it's Laali who kicked the scuttle off." She walks out with an empty bowl. Ruthu, scampers towards the scene keeping down her basket in a furrow to hold and close the eyes of calf. Mother begins her utmost joyful work with all the flair and dexterity, with the ritual of a splash to the udder. I make my way towards the lotus pond amidst the turbulent wind. Mothi overtakes me again.

www.ingramcontent.com/pod-product-compliance
Lightning Source LLC
LaVergne TN
LVHW041515170726
843492LV00005B/1520